Papatango Theatre Compan

The world premiere of the wi
2019 Papatango New Writing

SHOOK

by Samuel Bailey

Shook was first produced by Papatango Theatre Company on a national tour in 2019.

Shook Tour Dates

Southwark Playhouse, London
30 October–23 November 2019
Press night: 1 November
www.southwarkplayhouse.co.uk
Box Office: 020 7407 0234

The Hope Street Theatre, Liverpool
26 November 2019
www.hopestreettheatre.com
Box Office: 0344 561 0622

Theatr Clwyd, Mold
27–28 November 2019
www.theatrclwyd.com
Box Office: 01352 701521

Stephen Joseph Theatre, Scarborough
30 November 2019
www.sjt.uk.com
Box Office: 01723 370541

Marlowe Studio, Canterbury
4–7 December 2019
www.marlowetheatre.com
Box Office: 01227 787787

SHOOK

by Samuel Bailey

Cast

Jonjo	**Josef Davies**
Cain	**Josh Finan**
Grace	**Andrea Hall**
Riyad	**Ivan Oyik**

Director	**George Turvey**
Set and Costume Designer	**Jasmine Swan**
Lighting Designer	**Johanna Town**
Music and Sound Designer	**Richard Hammarton**
Producer	**Chris Foxon**
Fight Director	**Tim Klotz**
Assistant Director	**Lisa Diveney**
Assistant Lighting Designer	**Jack Wills**
Production Manager	**Marco Savo**
Stage Manager	**Jo Alexander**
Technical Assistant Stage Manager	**Tommaso Gobbi**
Costume Supervisor	**Megan Rarity**

The performance lasts approximately 90 minutes.

There will be no interval.

Cast and Creative Team

Josef Davies | Jonjo

Theatre includes: *Hangmen* (Royal Court Theatre/ West End), *The 306* (National Theatre of Scotland) and *Junkyard* (Headlong).

Film includes: *1917, The King, Dumbo, Undercliffe* and *The Limehouse Golem*.

Television includes: *Chernobyl, World on Fire, Silent Witness, Shakespeare and Hathaway, The Bisexual, Curfew, Call the Midwife* and *Uncle*.

Josh Finan | Cain

Theatre includes: *Romeo and Juliet, Macbeth* and *The Merry Wives of Windsor* (RSC), *The Nutcracker* (Theatr Clwyd), *Champ* (Tobacco Factory Theatres), *E15* (Lung Theatre/Northern Stage), *The Barricade* (Theatre503), *Pancake Day* (Bunker Theatre) and *Dolly Wants To Die* (Lung Theatre/Edinburgh Festival).

Film includes: *Surge, Hellboy* and *The Current War*.

Television includes *Guerilla*.

Andrea Hall | Grace

Theatre includes: *Ares* (VAULT Festival), *The Wild Duck* (Almeida Theatre), *The Notebook of Trigorin* (Finborough Theatre), *Hyacinth Blue* (Clean Break), *Talkin' Loud* (Theatre503), *Abena's Stupidest Mistake* (Talawa), *Parting Shots* (Bootleg Theatre), *Large Tales* (Nottingham Playhouse), *The Palace of Fear* (Leicester Haymarket) and *Johnny Dollar* (Bloomsbury Theatre).

Film includes: *The Child in Time*.

Television includes: *Broadchurch, Flack, Humans, Unforgotten, Casualty, Joe All Alone, Apple Tree House, Trauma, Doctors, Thirteen* and *Hood Documentary*.

Ivan Oyik | Riyad

Ivan graduated from Guildford School of Acting this summer.

Theatre includes: *Blue Orange* (Birmingham Rep, for which he was nominated for *The Stage* Debut Award for Best Actor in a Play) and *Red Pitch* (Ovalhouse).

Television includes *Doctors*.

Samuel Bailey | Playwright

Samuel was born in London and raised in the West Midlands. He began writing plays in Bristol and developed work with Bristol Old Vic, Tobacco Factory Theatres and Theatre West before moving back to London. He is an alumnus of the Old Vic 12 and Orange Tree Writers' Collective. *Shook* was originally supported by the MGCfutures bursary programme, and will be his debut full production.

George Turvey | Director

George co-founded Papatango in 2007 and became the sole Artistic Director in January 2013. Credits as director include: *Hanna* (Papatango, UK tour), *The Annihilation of Jessie Leadbeater* (Papatango at ALRA), *After Independence* (Papatango at Arcola Theatre, 2016 Alfred Fagon Audience Award, and BBC Radio 4), *Leopoldville* (Papatango at Tristan Bates Theatre) and *Angel* (Papatango at Pleasance London/Tristan Bates Theatre).

George trained as an actor at the Academy of Live and Recorded Arts (ALRA) and has appeared on stage and screen throughout the UK and internationally, including the lead roles in the world première of Arthur Miller's *No Villain* (Old Red Lion Theatre/Trafalgar Studios) and *Batman Live* World Arena Tour. As a dramaturg, he has led the development of all of Papatango's productions. He is the co-author of *Being a Playwright: A Career Guide for Writers*.

Jasmine Swan | Set and Costume Designer

Jasmine trained at Liverpool Institute for Performing Arts, where she also received the Ede & Ravenscroft Prize for Creative and Technical Excellence (2016). Jasmine designs for theatre, opera, dance and site-specific events. She was multiple nominated for Best Designer in *The Stage* Debut Awards 2018, for her designs at Theatre503, Finborough Theatre, Arcola Theatre and Brighton Rialto. Her set design for *Chutney* (Bunker Theatre) was nominated for an Off West End Award (2018) and featured on the SBTD Staging Places online exhibition for Prague Quadrennial 2018/19. She was a finalist in the Linbury Prize for Stage Design 2017, working with Phoenix Dance Theatre at West Yorkshire Playhouse. She was the Laboratory Associate Designer for Nuffield Southampton Theatres in 2017/18.

Credits as designer include: *Hanna* (Papatango at Arcola Theatre/national tour), *Scoring A Century* (British Youth Opera at The Peacock), *Eden* (Hampstead Theatre), *Women In Power* (Nuffield Southampton Theatres/Oxford Playhouse), *Armadillo* (Yard Theatre), *Sonny* (Arts Educational Schools), *Chutney* (Flux Theatre at Bunker Theatre, nominated for the Off West End Award for Best Set Design), *The Tide Jetty* (Eastern Angles), *Hyem* and *The Amber Trap* (Theatre503), *Sex Sex Men Men* (Yard Theatre, nominated for the Off West End Award for Idea Category), *Son of Rambow* (The Other Palace), *Lost Boys* and *SummerFest* (National Youth Theatre at Unity Theatre/Bunker Theatre), *Medusa* (Nuffield Southampton Theatre Studio), *Sleuth* (ZoieLogic Dance Theatre), *Much Ado About Nothing*, *Dungeness* and *Love and Information* (Nuffield Southampton Youth Theatre), *Cabaret* (Westminster School), *The Passing of the Third Floor Back* (Finborough Theatre), *The Sleeper* (Brighton Rialto), *Who's Afraid Of The Working Class?* (Unity Theatre) and *The Wonderful World of Dissocia* (Liverpool Playhouse Studio). www.jasmineswan.com

Johanna Town | Lighting Designer

Johanna has designed the lighting for numerous major theatre and opera companies both in the UK and internationally, including: National Theatre, Royal Shakespeare Company, West Yorkshire Playhouse, Sheffield Theatres, Royal Exchange Theatre, Manchester, and Chichester Festival Theatre, to name but a few, as well as productions in the West End, on Broadway, and abroad. She has designed over fifty productions for the Royal Court Theatre.

Her most recent productions include: *Two Ladies* (Bridge Theatre), *Some Like it Hiphop* (Zoonation), *Butterfly Lion, The Watsons* and *The Norman Conquests* (Chichester Festival Theatre), *Fracked!* (Jonathan Church Productions), *Rutherford & Son* and *Julius Caesar* (Sheffield Theatres), *Miss Julie* and *Creditors* (Theatre by the Lake/Jermyn Street Theatre), and *Frankenstein* and *Guys & Dolls* (Royal Exchange Theatre, Manchester).

Johanna is an Associate Artist for Theatre503, the Chair of the Association of Lighting Designers and was made a Fellow of Guildhall School of Music and Drama for her contribution to lighting design in theatre. This is her fourth production for Papatango following *Tomcat, Orca* and *Trestle* (2015, 2016 and 2017 Papatango New Writing Prize winners, all at Southwark Playhouse).

Richard Hammarton | Music and Sound Designer

Theatre includes: *Valued Friends* (Rose Theatre, Kingston), *Chiaroscuro* (Bush Theatre), *Red Dust Road* (National Theatre Scotland), *Ghosts, Love from a Stranger, Dealer's Choice* and *Someone Who'll Watch Over Me* (Royal & Derngate Theatres), *Wolfie* and *In The Event Of Moone Disaster* (Theatre503), *Princess & The Hustler* (Eclipse Theatre Company), *Lost Paradise* (New Visual Paradigm), *Under Milk Wood* (Northern Stage), *Women In Power* (Nuffield Southampton Theatres), *Describe the Night, Deposit* and *Sunspots* (Hampstead Theatre), *Out of Sight* (fanSHEN tour), *Jekyll and Hyde* (Touring Consortium Theatre Company), *Burning Doors* (Belarus Free Theatre), *Girls* (HighTide), *The Weir* (English Touring Theatre), *As You Like It* and *An Inspector Calls* (Theatre by the Lake), *Traitor* (Pilot Theatre), *Faust x2* (The Watermill Theatre), *Dirty Great Love Story* (Arts Theatre), *Assata Taught Me* and *Comrade Fiasco* (Gate Theatre), *Low Level Panic* (Orange Tree Theatre), *Luv* (Park Theatre), *Much Ado About Nothing* and *Jumpy* (Theatr Clwyd), *Linda* (Royal Court Theatre), *The Crucible, Brilliant Adventures, Dr Faustus* – winner of MEN Best Design Award – and *Edward II* (Royal Exchange Theatre, Manchester), *A Number* (Nuffield Theatre/Young Vic), *Beached* (Marlowe Theatre/Soho Theatre), *Grimm Tales 2* (Bargehouse, Oxo Tower Wharf), *Ghost from a Perfect Place* and *The Pitchfork Disney* (Arcola Theatre), *The Crucible* (Old Vic Theatre), *Sizwe Bansi is Dead* (Theatre Royal Stratford East/UK tour), *Kingston 14* (Theatre Royal Stratford East), *Bandages* (TEG Productions), *The Last Summer* (Gate Theatre, Dublin), *Six Characters Looking for an Author* (Young Vic) and *Mudlarks* (Hightide/Theatre503/Bush Theatre).

This is Richard's sixth production for Papatango, following *Hanna* (UK tour), *Trestle, Orca* and *Tomcat* (Southwark Playhouse) and *After Independence* (Arcola Theatre).

Television credits include: *Ripper Street, No Win No Fee, Sex 'n' Death, Wipeout, The Ship* and *Agatha Christie's Marple*.

Radio credits include *The Effect*.

Orchestration work includes: *Agatha Christie's Marple* series 1 & 2, *Primeval, Jericho, If I Had You, Dracula, A History of Britain, Silent Witness, Dalziel and Pascoe, Alice Through the Looking Glass, The Nine Lives of Tomas Katz* and *Scenes of a Sexual Nature*.

Chris Foxon | Producer

Chris is Executive Director of Papatango. His productions with the company include: *The Funeral Director* (Papatango New Writing Prize 2018, Southwark Playhouse/UK tour), *Hanna* (Arcola Theatre/UK tour), *Trestle* (Papatango New Writing Prize 2017, Southwark Playhouse), *Orca* (Papatango New Writing Prize 2016, Southwark Playhouse), *After Independence* (Arcola Theatre, 2016 Alfred Fagon Audience Award; BBC Radio 4), *Tomcat* (Papatango New Writing Prize 2015, Southwark Playhouse), *Coolatully* (Papatango New Writing Prize 2014, Finborough Theatre), *Unscorched* (Papatango New Writing Prize 2013, Finborough Theatre), and *Pack* and *Everyday Maps for Everyday Use* (Papatango New Writing Prize 2012, Finborough Theatre). He designed and launched GoWrite, Papatango's participation and engagement programme, and instigated the Resident Playwright and WriteWest playwriting development programmes.

Other productions include: *The Transatlantic Commissions* (Old Vic Theatre), *Donkey Heart* (Old Red Lion Theatre and Trafalgar Studios), *The Fear of Breathing* (Finborough Theatre; transferred in a new production to the Akasaka Red Theatre, Tokyo), *The Keepers of Infinite Space* (Park Theatre), *Happy New* (Trafalgar Studios), *Tejas Verdes* (Edinburgh Festival) and *The Madness of George III* (Oxford Playhouse).

Chris has lectured at the Royal Central School of Speech and Drama and the Universities of Northampton, Oxford and York. He is the co-author of *Being a Playwright: A Career Guide for Writers*.

Lisa Diveney | Assistant Director

Lisa trained as an actor at the Royal Welsh College of Music and Drama. She is currently Emerging Director at National Theatre Wales and a member of the Young Vic Directors Programme.

Assistant Directing credits include: *For All I Care* (National Theatre Wales) and *The Lucky Spot* (Royal Welsh College of Music and Drama).

Lisa has worked extensively as an actress. Recent theatre includes: *The Seagull* (Regent's Park Open Air Theatre) and *Donkey Heart* (Trafalgar Studios). Recent television includes *Harlots* and *Grantchester*.

Jack Wills | Assistant Lighting Designer

Jack graduated from Guildhall School of Music & Drama in July 2018.

Theatre as lighting designer includes: *Romeo and Juliet* (York Theatre Royal), *Robin Hood* (Theatre Peckham), *Kids Play* and *The Good Scout* (Above The Stag Theatre), *Boy Under The Christmas Tree* (King's Head Theatre), *Days of Significance* and *The Glove Thief* (ALRA London), *Annie* (Alban Arena), *Pericles* (Chateau Valtice Theatre, Czechia) and *Buckets* (Abbey Theatre).

He was Associate Lighting Designer at Alexandra Palace Theatre as part of London Fashion Week 2019, and is also the lead of the Association of Lighting Designers' Student Committee. This is his first production with Papatango.

Megan Rarity | Costume Supervisor

Megan trained at Arts University Bournemouth in Costume for Performance Design.

Theatre includes: *Hedda Gabler* (Sherman Theatre), *Valued Friends* (Rose Theatre Kingston), *Midsummer Night Party* (Old Vic Theatre), *The Audience* and *A Streetcar Named Desire* (Nuffield Southampton Theatres), *Dead Dog in a Suitcase (and other love songs)* (Kneehigh/world tour), *Blood Knot, Mayfly, Utility* and Directors' Festival Season: *Misterman, End of Hope, Albert's Boy, Even Stillness Breathes Slowly Against a Brick Wall* and *Wasted* (Orange Tree Theatre), *West Side Story* (Hartshorn-Hook Productions), *Eden* (Hampstead Theatre), *Eugenius!* (The Other Palace), *Ubu Karaoke* (Kneehigh), *Blueberry Toast* (Soho Theatre), *Beauty and the Beast* (Watersmeet Theatre), *Tryst* (Tabard Theatre), *Insignificance* (Arcola Theatre), *Zigger Zagger* (National Youth Theatre/Wilton's Music Hall), *Oklahoma!* (Bennet Memorial Diocesan School), *Posh* (Pleasance Theatre), *Dorian Grey* and *Lizzie the Pirate* (White Horse Theatre Company) and *The Tempest* (The Print Room).

Film includes *Carmilla*.

Production Acknowledgements

2019 Papatango New Writing Prize Reading Team | **Olu Alakija, Safaa Benson-Effiom, Kate Brower, Michael Byrne, Bridie Donaghy, Karis Halsall, Richard Hammarton, Rebecca Hill, Clive Judd, Jonny Kelly, Shabnom Khanom, Alice Kornitzer, Emily Lunnon, Katherine Nesbit, Callie Nestleroth, John Roberts, Harriet Sambrook, Blythe Stewart, Krystal Sweedman, Roisin Symes, Emma Wilkinson** and **Matt Woodhead**

Image Design | **Rebecca Pitt**

Image Photography | **Michael Wharley**

Production Photography | **The Other Richard**

Press Representation | **Kate Morley PR**

Shook was originally developed by Papatango with the following cast: **Anton Cross, Josh Finan, Danny Kirrane** and **Sharlene Whyte**

Many thanks to the 2019 Papatango New Writing Prize's generous supporters: Arts Council England; Backstage Trust; Boris Karloff Charitable Foundation; Cockayne – Grants for the Arts and The London Community Foundation; Foyle Foundation; Garrick Charitable Trust; Golsoncott Foundation; the Harold Hyam Wingate Foundation and the Leche Trust.

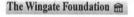

We are very grateful to our post-show event partners: Bounce Back, Key4Life and Switchback.

bounce back.

Bounce Back is a training charity and employer with centres in a number of prisons and communities. It supports people from prison into jobs, successfully helping them avoid going back to prison. Its professional decorating team work around London and it also supports people into work with several construction companies. Bounce Back is also partnered with the Metropolitan Police Divert Project focused on young people. Social mobility is at its heart; we welcome everyone to find out more, volunteer or simply support us.

Key4Life's mission is to reduce youth reoffending through a ground-breaking rehabilitation programme for young men (18 to 30) in prison or at risk of going to prison and children (10 to 17) caught up in gang and knife crime. Key4Life works with some of the most disadvantaged young men by supporting and empowering them to secure employment and reintegrate into society on a positive path away from crime. The cost of one participant in the Key4Life programme is £5,000 versus the average annual cost of a prison place in England and Wales of £37,000.

SWITCHBACK

Switchback is an award-winning charity based in London supporting 18- to 30-year-old prison-leavers to make real, lasting change. Switchback Mentors provide intensive one-to-one support either side of the prison gate, alongside real work training after release, enabling Trainees to find a way out of the justice system and build a stable, rewarding life they can be proud of. Switchback Trainees are five times less likely to re-offend than the national average. 84% of Trainees that complete Switchback move into employment, while 58% have reached Switchback's benchmark of real, lasting change, making a fundamental shift in mindset and lifestyle.

PAPAtango

Papatango was founded to champion the best new playwriting talent in the UK and Ireland. We discover and launch playwrights through free, open application opportunities. Our motto is simple: all you need is a story.

Our flagship programme is the Papatango New Writing Prize, the UK's first and still only annual award to guarantee an emerging playwright a full production, publication, 10% of the gross box office, and an unprecedented £6000 commission for a second play. Prize-winners have transferred worldwide, received great acclaim and awards, and risen to leading positions in theatre, film and TV.

The Prize is free to enter and assessed anonymously. All entrants receive personal feedback on their scripts, an unmatched commitment to supporting aspiring playwrights. 1,406 entries were received in 2019, meaning the Prize continues to receive more annual submissions than any other UK playwriting award – and yet is unique in giving feedback and support to all.

Papatango also run an annual Resident Playwright scheme, taking an emerging playwright through commissioning, development and production. It gives in-depth, sustained support to writers who might not otherwise be in a position to win the Prize, for lack of access to resources such as training, commissions or mentoring. Our Residents have toured the UK, adapted their work for radio, and transitioned to full-time careers as writers.

We use the astonishing success of the writers discovered and launched through these opportunities to inspire others that they too can make and enjoy top-class theatre.

GoWrite delivers an extensive programme of free playwriting opportunities for children and adults nationwide. Children in state schools write plays which are then professionally performed and published, while adults join workshops, complete six-month courses at a variety of regional venues culminating in free public performances, or access fortnightly one-to-one career advice sessions.

GoWrite delivers face-to-face training for over 2000 writers each year, not only free but with £5000 available in travel bursaries to enable anyone to access its opportunities.

This year we launched a new programme named WriteWest to build a playwriting ecosystem across South West England, in partnership with major venues throughout the region. It offers free playwriting courses in Taunton and Plymouth, culminating in free public showcases; a free producing course with £9000 in seed funding to support participants' new productions; and free workshops in libraries and state schools. Again, as well as being free, £5000 in travel bursaries make these accessible to all.

Writers discovered through these opportunities have won BAFTAs, Off West End, RNT Foundation Playwright and Alfred Fagon Awards, been nominated for the Susan Smith Blackburn Prize and Evening Standard Most Promising Playwright Award, and premiered in over twenty countries.

10% of seats at our productions are donated to charities for young people at risk of exclusion from the arts.

Our first book *Being a Playwright: A Career Guide for Writers* was published in 2018 and described as 'a phenomenon for playwriting good... a bible for playwrights' by award-winning writer and academic Steve Waters and as 'an excellent tool for playwrights' by Indhu Rubasingham, artistic director of the Kiln Theatre.

All Papatango's opportunities are free and entered anonymously, encouraging the best new talent regardless of background.

'Southwark Playhouse churn out arresting productions at a rate of knots' *Time Out*

Southwark Playhouse is all about telling stories and inspiring the next generation of storytellers and theatre makers. It aims to facilitate the work of new and emerging theatre practitioners from early in their creative lives to the start of their professional careers.

Through our schools work we aim to introduce local people at a young age to the possibilities of great drama and the benefits of using theatre skills to facilitate learning. Each year we engage with over 5,000 school pupils through free schools performances and long-term in school curriculum support.

Through our participation programmes we aim to work with all members of our local community in a wide ranging array of creative drama projects that aim to promote cohesion, build confidence and encourage a lifelong appreciation of theatre.

Our theatre programme aims to facilitate and showcase the work of some of the UK's best up and coming talent with a focus on reinterpreting classic plays and contemporary plays of note. Our two atmospheric theatre spaces enable us to offer theatre artists and companies the opportunity to present their first fully realised productions. Over the past 25 years we have produced and presented early productions by many aspiring theatre practitioners many of whom are now enjoying flourishing careers.

'A brand as quirky as it is classy' *The Stage*

For more information about our forthcoming season and to book tickets visit www.southwarkplayhouse.co.uk. You can also support us online by joining our Facebook and Twitter pages.

SHOOK

Samuel Bailey

To my Dad,
for the inspiration

Acknowledgements

Thank you to: Stella McCabe, Molly McCarthy, Nick Frankfort and everyone at MGC for being the first to believe in the play; Kate Byers, for reading every one of my first drafts; Anthony Horowitz, for his generosity and guidance; Joe Langdon, for his insight and advice; Steven Atkinson, for his helpful words when I got stuck; Rebecca Durbin, for her constant words of encouragement; Akiya Henry, Theo Ogundipe, Sharlene Whyte, Danny Kirrane and Anton Cross for their invaluable input; Josh Finan, Josef Davies, Ivan Oyik and Andrea Hall for being everything I had in my head and a little bit more; the Peggy Ramsay Foundation for helping me pay my rent; everyone at NHB and Southwark Playhouse for all their hard work; Kate Prentice and everyone at 42 for taking a punt on me; and Mum, for everything.

Special thanks to George Turvey and Chris Foxon for making it happen, what you do every year is unbelievable; and Jesse Jones, my theatre big brother, for showing me the way.

And the lads back home, who think theatre is rubbish, but are, in some form, in every play I've ever written.

S.B.

Characters

CAIN, *sixteen*
JONJO, *seventeen*
RIYAD, *sixteen*
GRACE, *late thirties*

Setting

A young offenders institute classroom. Bare, unloved.
A whiteboard.

Notes

(**,**) denotes a withholding of speech, an expression of
something without words.

(–) at the end of a sentence indicates the next line cutting in.

(…) indicates a trailing-off of thought or, in Jonjo's case,
a fluency interruption.

*This text went to press before the end of rehearsals and so may
differ slightly from the play as performed.*

ONE

CAIN *and* JONJO – *both in green tracksuits.* JONJO *has white, prison-issue daps on.* CAIN *his own trainers and a plastic rosary hung about his neck.*

CAIN, *a wiry bundle of energy, loiters at the door, peering through the small window.*

JONJO, *big and wounded, sits passively on a chair, waiting.*

CAIN. And you don't go in there, right? Nowhere round pool table. Not unless you want Saleem and his lot to slap you about and you don't want that, fucking believe me so just you steer clear altogether.

On twos you, yeah? Who do I know up there? You met Ryan Buckley? He's alright, la. Just don't say nothing to him about his eye, cus he's sensitive as fuck about it and he will smash yer head in.

What did you do to get in here, anyway?

JONJO. ,

CAIN. They moved me down from Glen Parva when it closed down. I was gonna get out but then this fucking prick Isan, Greek or summat he was, starts telling everyone he saw me crying after visits, telling every fucker he can that he saw me crying, which is bang out of order, there's some things you just don't joke about, so I boiled me kettle and stuck a load of sugar in it but this screw caught me with it just before I could chuck it in his face.

The fucking prick.

CAIN *goes back to the window, craning to see down the hall.*

He bangs on the door to get attention.

I haven't got all fucking day, like. Who's that? Zahid, you nonce. Zahid, Zahid. Zahid, in here.

You know they're doing carpentry? Fuck. I wish I was doing carpentry. *Apparently*, I can't be trusted around tools. That's what they said. It was one fucking screwdriver, lad. And they never even found it so how did they even know it was me who nicked it? They never. Could have been anyone but it's always me that gets picked on.

You don't think I was crying, do yer? I wasn't. And if I was it's only cus my sister had been and my nephew, right, her kid, who I've not actually ever met to be fair but that's beside the point, got diagnosed with this really rare type of brain thingy… whatever. So if I was, which I wasn't, then it was cus of that which is fucking fair enough if you ask –

The door partially opens, catching their attention.

It slams back again. The sound of a commotion filters through from the other side.

CAIN *rushes to watch.*

That's it, mate. Fucking have him. Go on, do him. John. Johnny. John. John. Ah, yer prick.

Broken up. See any of that? Always gets broken up in about two seconds. Was you even watching? Got to fight differently in here, la. Get in and do as much damage as you can, quick as possible, right? Biting, punching, kicking, fucking whatever. Like a whirlwind. I must have had fifty fights at Parva, at least. They were gonna star me up but then it closed down anyway and I got sent here.

He was never gonna win that. Johnny's all fucking show, man. I'd knock him out. You'd probably have him.

CAIN *pulls out a bag of sweets from his pocket.*

Mind you. He has done four years so he must have done something pretty fucking mad, like.

CAIN *offers a sweet to* JONJO.

JONJO *shakes his head.*

Suit yourself. You get any baccy in here? I'm dying for a ciggy, man.

They pay you for these, you know. Coming to these classes.
Fifty pence. Only reason I'm here. If this bird doesn't show
then whatever, like. I'm gonna get some Wine Gums. Or
Black Jacks. There's always loads of Black Jacks cus most
people don't like 'em, but I fucking love 'em.

It's gonna be a breeze, mate. New teacher, I heard. Bet you
I can make her cry. Not like full-on cry but you know when
their eyes get like all watery. Bet I can do that. At Parva
I made four teachers quit, they had to get the top lad down to
teach classes.

This your first time? I've been loads. Basically at home here.
They should fucking name the wing after me. The Cain
Walters Wing. Got a nice ring to it, eh?

CAIN *clicks his fingers in front of* JONJO.

Throws a sweet at him, it bounces off his head.

Yer gonna have to say something to someone… *sometime.*
I don't care if you don't wanna talk to me, whatever, but
some lads might think you're ignoring 'em and smash you
up anyway.

You thick or something? Don't matter to me but seems if
you're a mong you probably shouldn't be here. They've got
a whole special unit for window-lickers and that.

At Parva there was this one kid, what was he called, don't
matter, he got a tattoo right here on his head, cus he thought
it'd make him look hard but honestly it just made him look
a right twat, and they ended up just using it as a target when
they smacked him really –

JONJO. I m-miss my dog.

CAIN. Fuck me, it speaks. I was beginning to think maybe you
was foreign or summat. What did you say? Your dog? What
type of dog you got?

JONJO. ,

CAIN. I had a dog. A Staffy. Found him in someone's shed
fucking chained to the lawnmower. So, me and my mate
Danny went home and got the bolt cutters, cut the chain off

and set fire to the cunt's shed for a laugh. And as payback for him being a top dickhead and chaining the dog up in there. Took the dog home. Called him Thor. You know? Like off Marvel. Have you not seen *Thor: Ragnarok*? Mate. It's sick. You must have seen *Infinity War*. Fuck. Have you seen *Endgame*?

Kept him for three years, then he got like this lump in his neck and I couldn't afford the operation so the vet had to put him down. Little fucker.

Who's your PO? I got Herring. He's a fucking prick. I hate him.

RIYAD, *coiled like a spring, enters.*

CAIN *moves away instinctively – giving him space.*

RIYAD. What's your star sign?

CAIN. What?

RIYAD. Your star sign, blud. Aries and Capri-Sun and what not. All that shit.

CAIN. I dunno. Why?

RIYAD. When's your birthday?

CAIN. Twenty-fifth October.

RIYAD. October... October...

CAIN. Why? What does that make me?

RIYAD. I'm thinking.

CAIN. Dragon. I'm a dragon.

RIYAD. Nah, that's the fucking Chinese one. I don't even know, yano. Fuck's sake. They won't let me on a computer.

JONJO. S-scorpio.

RIYAD. Scorpio! Yeah, that's it – who the fuck is this?

CAIN. Dunno. He ain't said his name.

RIYAD. Have you asked him?

CAIN. Don't talk. Well, not really. He said summat about his dog a minute ago but he's been dead quiet. He's new.

RIYAD. What's a Scorpio, then? How'd you know it's October?

JONJO *shrugs*.

CAIN. Why'd you care, anyway?

RIYAD. I got a letter from my girl. She's fucking... talking about how she's a water sign and I'm Sagittarius and how our alignment is off or some bullshit. How Jamal's a Taurus, and they've been getting on good lately and they've got some mad Venus compatibility coming up.

CAIN. Right...

RIYAD. Know what I'm saying?

CAIN. I don't even know what a fucking Sagittarius is.

RIYAD. It's a star sign. I dunno, do I? It's like this weird... horse thing. Like, this bredder with horse legs, innit. I dunno. Some Harry Potter shit.

She says Cancer and Sagittarius should never be a match in love. Bonds aren't strong. And she needs time to think. She needs to *think*, bruv.

CAIN. Nothing good comes of that.

RIYAD. They won't let me use a computer or nothing cus I'm still on basic, innit.

She's talking about the moon passing through Jupiter and shit. What's Jupiter gotta do with me being with my girl, innit?

Fucking Jamal, he even thinks about going near my girl, I'll fucking wet him up, blud, swear down. I ain't got a visit from her for two weeks, still.

I always treated her good.

CAIN. When they move you off D-wing?

RIYAD. Last night. Put me in a new yard, innit cus the last one is still all smashed up, still. Left the letters from Serita on my bed.

CAIN (*to* JONJO). He's been on D-wing for two weeks. It's
     where they put you if you need to be taken off main and –

RIYAD. What you telling man my business for?

CAIN. Nah, I'm not, like.

RIYAD. What's your name, bruv?

JONJO. ,

RIYAD. Yo, what's your name, man?

     Is he tapped or something?

CAIN. He does look a bit like a spastic.

RIYAD (*to* JONJO). You want I can just call you Scorpio, innit,
     you don't wanna tell me your name.

CAIN. Why's no one ever given me a cool nickname?

RIYAD. Cus you're a fucking dickhead, bruv. Shut up. (*To*
     JONJO.) Come on, fam. What's your name? I asked you a
     question, innit. It's rude to ignore people.

JONJO. Jon... jo.

RIYAD. Jonjo?

JONJO. Yeah.

CAIN. Jonjo? What kinda name is that? Like... is it John, or Joe?
     Make your mind up. Sounds like a gypo name to me. Gypos
     call their kids like Jimmy Alan, or Toby Dean and shit –

RIYAD (*to* JONJO). This Scouse dickhead pissing you off, bruv?
     Shall we smash him up, yeah? He talks too much, innit.

CAIN. What?

RIYAD. Get you a name, innit. People wouldn't fuck around
     with you then.

CAIN. Leave it out, eh?

RIYAD. Honestly, you'd be doing a lot of man in here a favour.
     I'll hold the door, yeah, so no one can get in and you just
     raggo on him, yeah?

CAIN. Riyad, come on, mate...

RIYAD. I'm just joking, fuck. I got my mums coming this week, man. She'll be pissed if I got locked down again and I need her to speak to Serita for me. So none of you fuck around, you get me? Any of you get me in trouble you're dead, innit.

CAIN. Nice one, yeah...

RIYAD. What did I just say to you, blud?

CAIN *mimes zipping his lips. Peers through the window.*

How'd you know that shit about star signs and that?

JONJO. M-Mum likes horoscopes.

Like... what's in your future.

RIYAD. They tell your future?

JONJO. G-guess so.

RIYAD. Maybe my mums will know about this star-sign shit.

CAIN *gesturing outside.*

What, blud?

CAIN *points again.*

Don't be a waste, you can speak now, innit.

CAIN. I reckon this is her. Got to be. She's defo not a screw.

Oh, went the wrong way. Wrong classroom, you stupid bitch. We're in here. She's quite fit, actually.

RIYAD. We got a woman teacher, yeah?

CAIN. Yeah. She's talking to that fucking weapon, Jake.

Eh. Bagsy.

RIYAD. What?

CAIN. Bagsy. Shotgun. Whatever yous lot call it down here. I call bagsy. On her.

RIYAD *approaches the window.*

RIYAD. You can't fucking bagsy.

CAIN. I just did.

RIYAD. Well, you can't.

CAIN. Why not? I saw her. I called bagsy. That's how it works.

RIYAD. Cus I fucking say so. And anyway, if anyone's beating, it's me. I got the woman problems, innit.

RIYAD *pushes* CAIN *out of the way.*

Where? Bruv, she's ain't that peng, man. That one there? She's like a pencil, innit, straight up and down.

CAIN. I think she's tidy.

RIYAD. She ain't got no curves, bruv. Real women got shape. Big titties. She ain't got none of that.

CAIN. Curves. No curves. I don't give a shit. I haven't fucked a girl in fourteen months.

RIYAD. Fourteen months?

CAIN. He probably don't even know what a fanny looks like.

RIYAD. Then why would he be here, bruv? Think, man. Pikeys start young, yano.

JONJO. I'm not a p-p…

CAIN. I shagged my first girl when I was eleven.

RIYAD. Bullshit.

CAIN. I'm telling yer. She couldn't keep her hands off me.

RIYAD. Yeah? What was she called?

CAIN. ,

Stella.

RIYAD. Stella. Bullshit, bruv. You might have had your first can of Stella when you was eleven, but you didn't fuck no girl called Stella.

Now she's gone into Jake's office. This is long. If they ain't starting this soon, I'm out, man. Fuck their classes.

CAIN. Bet she's fucking Jake.

RIYAD. Do you ever shut up, man? I'm fucking glad my pad's not next to yours…

CAIN. You're gonna have to have Jake's sloppy seconds.

RIYAD. Doubt it.

CAIN. Yeah, bet he gets to fuck all the new birds. Like a job interview.

RIYAD. Nah, it ain't like that.

CAIN. That's what I'd do.

RIYAD. They're just filling in some forms or something. They ain't fucking.

CAIN. How'd you know?

RIYAD. Trust me, innit.

CAIN. You don't know shit.

RIYAD. I know more than you.

CAIN. Bollocks. You don't know shit.

RIYAD. Jake's a batty boy.

CAIN. What? Fuck off.

RIYAD. Swear down.

CAIN. Nah. Serious?

RIYAD. Yeah, man.

CAIN. Nah.

RIYAD. *Swear down.*

CAIN. He don't look like one.

RIYAD. Well, he is.

CAIN. Fuck. That's rank. He touched me when I went mental by canteen last month. I've probably got like AIDS or something now.

RIYAD. You ain't got AIDS.

CAIN. He's probably gonna try and bum me.

RIYAD. Rah. Think Jake can do better than a scrawny rat like you, innit.

CAIN. What, like you?

RIYAD. Suck your mum, man. I ain't no chi-chi. I'm just saying, innit. Jake's alright. Helping me with my Maths GCSE.

CAIN. What? They're letting you do a GCSE? Like, a proper one?

RIYAD. Yeah, man.

CAIN. What the fuck? They won't let me do a GCSE.

RIYAD. I'm smart, still. Got a brain for numbers, innit, that's what they said. From counting all them boxes.

Missed out on doing my module-one geometry cus I was on D, but now I'm back on the unit. About to make equilateral triangles my *bitch*.

CAIN. I'm smart.

RIYAD. Yeah? What's a decimal then, bruv?

CAIN. A what?

RIYAD. What's a fraction?

CAIN (*grabbing his crotch*). Fraction this, dickhead.

RIYAD. I heard you can't even read.

CAIN. Who told you I can't read?

RIYAD. Bare people.

CAIN. I can fucking read. I ain't a pikey. (*To* JONJO.) You doing GCSEs?

JONJO *shrugs*.

I could have got GCSEs if I wanted 'em. I was the smartest kid in Glen Parva. All them used to ask me for the answers. Said I should be the one teaching the classes.

RIYAD. Yeah, right.

CAIN. What you doing here with us, then, if you're so clever? Why ain't you on fucking *University Challenge* or whatever? Why you doing some shit parenting classes with us for?

RIYAD. I dunno. Just sounded interesting, innit. Different.

(*To* JONJO.) What you saying, big man? What you doing here?

JONJO. Didn't know we had to… come to classes.

RIYAD. Yeah, man. You have to go bare classes here. Well, you're supposed to. If they got the people to bring you to and from, innit.

CAIN. I thought it would just be dossing around. Going gym, getting henny.

RIYAD. Bruv, you couldn't do ten press-ups. Getting *henny*.

CAIN. Eh, fuck off, lad. I can do *fifty* – I could *a hundred* press-ups. Someone count.

CAIN *starts doing press-ups*.

RIYAD (*to* JONJO). You got a kid, then?

JONJO. S-sort of.

RIYAD. Sort of? How's that work, then?

JONJO. ,

RIYAD. Your business, blud. How he ever got any girl to fuck him, I don't know.

CAIN. Fuck. You. Nine… Ten…

RIYAD. I got one already. Marcus. Yeah. My little soldier, innit. But like… I'm not with my baby mum and it's all like this pure madness. Gonna change that though, when I get out. Know what I mean? Be there for him, innit.

CAIN (*jumping up*). What you gonna do with a Maths GCSE, anyway?

RIYAD. Dunno yet, still.

CAIN. Exactly.

RIYAD. I know I'm gonna be my own boss. I ain't going back on road after this. Proper. Legit. After I'm done with this Jake says I can take a Business BTEC or do A levels and then go uni, even.

CAIN. Surprised he can say all that when he's got his tongue in your arsehole.

RIYAD (*standing*). You fucking what?

CAIN. Go on, then. See where it gets yer. See what happens. Straight back to D-wing.

RIYAD. Don't test me, blud.

CAIN. Whatever.

RIYAD (*moving towards* CAIN). Keep talking, yeah.

GRACE *enters*.

RIYAD *and* CAIN *bristle*.

GRACE. Hi. Hi, everyone. Thanks for waiting. There were a few things to, you know, go through. My name's Grace. Nice to meet you all.

(*To* RIYAD.) Shall we take a seat?

RIYAD. Nah, you know what, fuck this, man. I'm gonna go see if Jake will let me use his computer.

(*To* GRACE *in the doorway*.) Get out my fucking way.

GRACE (*stepping to the side*). Mr Bradley is outside if you want to…

RIYAD *slams the door behind him*.

Leave.

CAIN. You should fucking write him up for that. Having a strop. Being aggressive, weren't he? He's already on thin ice with his PO, get him fucking kicked out. He's a Block-15 boy, right, he's had his pad moved twice already cus of them E3 lads that was down the wing. Akeem and that.

(*To* JONJO.) Fucking kicked off, big time, right. Proper mad shit. Not allowed nowhere near each other now, separate rec times, separate scran, the lot.

GRACE. He can leave if he wants to. That's fine.

CAIN. Just saying. You want to watch him. They're fucking mad cunts, the lot of 'em. That fucking Akeem. Telling yer.

GRACE. Why don't we just sit down? Don't worry about what's going on out there.

CAIN. Nah, sack this off. Fuck your Black Jacks. If he's going, I ain't staying in here, everyone will think I'm a prick. He's probably already out there spreading shit about me.

(*To* JONJO.) Eh, listen, you wouldn't have, you know... started, would yer? When Riyad was having a laugh. You wouldn't have done nothing?

GRACE. You're more than welcome to stay but if you're going to leave, then leave. Or sit down.

CAIN. I'm going. (*To* JONJO.) Gotta stick up for yourself, though. In here. If you don't it'll just make the time you got seem like fucking forever. How long are you here for?

GRACE. Mr Walters.

CAIN. Alright, fuck me. (*To* JONJO.) Remember what I said about Ryan Buckley, innit. The eye thing. Saw him eating metal screws in joinery once. He's not right in the head. And don't eat the rice pudding, yeah?

CAIN *exits.*

JONJO *takes out a sweet. Unwraps it and chews it slowly.*

JONJO *gets up and picks up a chair. Puts it down next to* GRACE. *Returns to his seat.*

GRACE. Thank you. You must be Jonjo?

JONJO. Y-yes, miss.

GRACE. Would you like to stay?

JONJO *nods.*

Good. We can be new together. You're going to be having a baby daughter, right? Exciting. Lots to look forward to. Shall we get started?

TWO

RIYAD *and* JONJO.

On the whiteboard – evidence of a class they just had.

A baby doll in the corner.

RIYAD. Maths I get, innit. Two plus two. Six times seven. Two, three, five, seven, eleven, thirteen, seventeen. Know what they are? Prime numbers. All *day*.

But this shit.

I'm just gonna say it. You can't teach how to be a parent. You just can't. You either got it in you or you don't, innit. That's why it's called the maternal *instinct*.

I'm a businessman. I'm here to provide. That's my job.

JONJO. I thought it was… okay.

RIYAD. I go out, earn the money. I'm alright with that, still. It worked for thousands of years like that. Why we got to change it now?

JONJO. I w-wouldn't mind.

RIYAD. Staying at home?

JONJO. Yeah.

RIYAD. You do you, innit. Not for me.

Why you keep calling her 'miss' for, anyway?

JONJO. She's a t-teacher.

RIYAD. Bruv, you ain't in school, you in pen. Lucky it's just me in here with you, innit. Don't be calling her *miss*, mans will think you're soft. She ain't your friend, bruv.

Can you see her nipples through her shirt?

JONJO. W-what?

RIYAD. I swear down I could see her nipples through her shirt. I'm going mad in here.

CAIN *enters, hyped. He's got a lollipop in his mouth.*

CAIN. Johnny Corbett's on suicide watch. Johnny Corbett's on suicide watch. Johnny's on fucking suicide watch.

RIYAD. Swear down?

CAIN. Swear *down*.

RIYAD. What happened?

CAIN. He's on obs. Tried to fucking top himself.

RIYAD. He wouldn't do that.

CAIN. Well, he did, so…

RIYAD. You're lying.

CAIN. Ask yer boyfriend Jake if you don't believe me. I seen his wrists. They carried him right by my pad on the way to the ozzy. Apparently sharpened his toothbrush, right, and… (*Motions dragging up his wrists.*) Now they got him on twenty-four-hour watch. That's why I'm late, they didn't have no one to bring me down here.

Has she gone already? I thought she'd be late again. Fuck. What did I miss?

JONJO. It's on the b-board.

RIYAD. What a pussy'ole. What's he done that for?

CAIN. Zahid reckons it's cus they were gonna let him out after Christmas. That's why he keeps kicking off with everyone. That's why he had that scrap with Leon in the gym. Why he won't go to none of his classes no more. Mostly just sits in his room. I walked past there last week and he was just sitting on his bed with his pillowcase on his head. It was dead weird.

RIYAD. He should be fucking happy. He's getting out.

CAIN. He went long-ways. That's not messing about, la.

RIYAD. What?

CAIN. Sideways for attention, longways to get the job done. *Guns for show, knives for a pro.*

(*Rolls up his sleeve.*) Check it. I done these in Parva.

RIYAD. The fuck is that on your arm, bruv?

CAIN. I'm not a fucking weirdo or nothing. Sideways, see?
I was bored. Locked up twenty-two hours a day in that place.
No staff to take you nowhere, way worse than here. I just
needed some *drama*, man. I needed to get fucking out.

RIYAD. Bet he's all cushty now. Lying up in bed, chilling out.

CAIN. Think he like nearly died.

RIYAD. Good. If he comes back on the wing, I'll mash him up.
Scared cus he's getting out? That's a fucking insult to me.
He can do my time, innit. And I can go home.

JONJO (*to* CAIN). You could go... and visit him.

CAIN. Who?

JONJO. Your mate. It makes you feel better getting visitors in
the h-hospital. When something like that has happened.

CAIN. Johnny? He's not my fucking mate. He's a *bag*head.

JONJO. Oh. Right.

CAIN. Don't go round telling people he's my mate. Cus he's
not. I just thought someone should tell the two of yers.

RIYAD (*to* CAIN). Give man a Chupa Chup.

CAIN. I've only got one left.

RIYAD. Lucky I'm only asking for one then, still.

CAIN. Green's me favourite.

RIYAD. And?

CAIN (*handing it over*). What you still doing here?

RIYAD. Waiting for transport, innit.

CAIN. What you been doing?

RIYAD. She's just been showing us videos of breastfeeding,
innit. To, like... show us what we're missing while we're
in here.

CAIN. No fucking way!

RIYAD. Yeah, that was today's class. Just watching videos of all, like… women and how they do it and how they hold the baby. And formula and that.

CAIN. Were they proper out? Has she left the tape behind? Fucking Johnny Corbett. I hope he does fucking die.

RIYAD. I'm just fucking with you. Obviously we didn't watch no video with bare titties and that. It was nothing.

My man here knows his shit, though. Answering all the questions. Burping, feeding, changing nappies. Proper little daddy day care, innit, bruv?

CAIN. How's he know how to do all that?

RIYAD. I dunno. Ask him.

JONJO. I've got a little sister.

CAIN. Told you he was a gypo, didn't I? Bet he's got loads of 'em. That's cheating. Course you're gonna know how to look after a kid if you've had to bring up your own brothers and sisters cus your dad's having a pissed-up scrap in a muddy field with some other dickhead who lives in a caravan.

JONJO. I didn't… I'm n-n-not…

CAIN. *I didn't, I'm n-n-n-not.*

JONJO. Don't…

CAIN. Don't what? What you gonna do?

RIYAD. Fifty pence he caves your head in.

CAIN. Fuck off, he will.

JONJO. Just l-leave me alone.

CAIN. Ooh, I think your tampon fell out. I'm only having a laugh.

JONJO. I haven't done anything to you.

CAIN. You're just there, though, aren't yer? Being all fucking spazzy.

JONJO. I'm not… a… a…

CAIN. Yeah I know what you're not. You say that loads. I just want to know what you *are*, innit.

JONJO. What… I am?

CAIN. *Who.*

JONJO. I said. I t-told you.

CAIN. Told us your name. Which means pretty much fuck-all. Said some other weird shit about your dog. Don't know one fucking thing about yer apart from that.

I can't be mates with someone I don't know. I ain't never met yer, I ain't never seen you before. No one has. And I've asked. Everyone. Everyone on my floor. Everyone on two. No one knows yer. Not John, not Zahid. Not even Leon and he's been near enough every place there is to go.

You ain't been in before and you won't tell no one what you done. And you say he's good with kids, yeah? Maybe you should be on D. Maybe he's a fucking nonce.

JONJO. N-no.

RIYAD. Mans was holding that doll suspiciously tight.

CAIN. He fucking is. That's disgusting, that is.

JONJO (*standing*). I'm not.

CAIN. What you standing up for?

JONJO. I don't want to you t-telling people –

CAIN. I don't want people knowing I go classes with a nonce. Yer secret's safe with me.

JONJO. It's not a secret.

CAIN. Yer proud of it? Dirty bastard.

JONJO. What? No. Of course not. Th-that's not what I said.

RIYAD (*laughing*). Come on, man. Allow it.

CAIN. I just want to know what he's standing up for? What you standing up for? I'll straight-up jaw you, kid. I don't give a fuck how big you are. I'll climb up there and kick yer teeth right down the back of yer throat.

RIYAD. Just tell us something, bruv. And not something weird. Like… where you from, man?

JONJO. Me?

RIYAD. Yeah, you.

CAIN. *You talking to me?*

JONJO. Why's that... important?

RIYAD. Why's it important? Just is. So you can be verified, blud. So people on the unit know who they're spending their days around, you get me? So we know who you are.

JONJO. I'm from B-Bromley.

RIYAD. Bromley mandem, yeah?

JONJO. I went to Ravensbourne. To school.

RIYAD. There you go. Mans went to Ravensbourne. I think I was linking some girl from there once, yano. Ciara. Sarah. Something.

Who's your boys? Who'd you hang around with?

JONJO. I don't go out much.

RIYAD. Big man just stays inside and plays his Xbox. Smart, innit. Obviously somehow manages to do something very fucking illegal, but that's for another day, still.

CAIN. Could still be a kiddy-fiddler. But like, on his computer. I bet he got caught with like thousands of pictures of kids doing fucking –

JONJO. I don't have a computer –

CAIN. Saving up for a trip to Thailand. Or Cambodia or wherever it is you nonces go.

JONJO. I said I'm not! L-leave me alone!

CAIN (*singing*). We're all going on a nonce-y holiday, loads more nonce-ing for a week or two –

JONJO *exits*.

RIYAD. Look what you done, you dickhead.

CAIN. Whatever, man. If he can't take a fucking joke.

RIYAD. What you giving him such a hard time for?

CAIN. Have I just had a stroke and woke up in fucking Legoland? What are you? His fairy godmother?

RIYAD. I'm just saying lay off, innit.

CAIN. What you sticking up for him for?

RIYAD. I ain't. I'm sticking up for you. Keep baiting him, blud, he's gonna go off. He's got that look, trust. I don't wanna get into no shit.

CAIN. *Got that look.* I've got that look. I'll fucking go off.

RIYAD. They gonna be piling in here, scraping you off the floor, fam. Believe.

CAIN. Whatever, man. I'm like the Terminator. I just keep coming. I'm indestructible.

RIYAD. Bruv, the Terminator dies. Goes in all that lava shit.

CAIN. Well. Sort of. In *Terminator 2*, he does. *Judgment Day*. But he comes back, don't he? The timelines are a bit all over the place, like, to be fair.

Ain't you curious? We could be hanging out with a paedo.

RIYAD. He ain't one of them, man.

A silence ensues.

RIYAD *looks out the window, unwraps a Refresher bar.*

Why don't your mum come and visit?

CAIN. My mum?

RIYAD. Yeah.

CAIN. Why'd you wanna know that for?

RIYAD. Maybe I'm curious about you. I ain't never seen no one come for you, innit. I know you ain't from down here still, but you think someone would come visit you once in a while.

CAIN. Guess not.

RIYAD. She like… working or some shit?

CAIN. Nah.

RIYAD. So, where's your mums at?

CAIN. I ain't got one, alright?

RIYAD. What?

CAIN. What I said. Ain't got one.

RIYAD. What d'you mean, you ain't got one? Everyone's got
a mum. Fair enough if your old man's fucked off, that's
normal, innit, but your mum…

CAIN. Don't know what to tell yer, la. I'm a miracle baby.
Grew me in a lab. It's why I'm better than you at everything.

RIYAD. Ain't she like worried about you or nothing?

CAIN (*shrugs*). Dunno. You'd have to find her and ask her.

I miss me bike. Spraypainted it all, right, matte-black. Disc
brakes. Front suspension. Proper rapid on it. No one could
catch me. Not even bizzies. I miss going fishing and that.
You ever been?

Go down the river, take your rod, few bevvies. Chill. Not
bothering no one, getting in no trouble. Have a few bifters,
like? On my phone I got a picture of me with a thirty-pound
carp. Fucking beast of a fish, he was.

RIYAD. Wasn't it all slimy and shit?

CAIN. Nah. Not really. Scales are smooth, like.

RIYAD. I don't really get fishing.

CAIN. That's cus you're from London. Fuck-all places to fish.

RIYAD. Nah, but like… how'd you win? Like, who's it
against? The fish? Don't seem fair. Man versus a fish.

CAIN. Nah, that like, comes from the weighing and that. Who's
got the biggest. Anyway, you're missing the point. It's just
about chilling, right. Having your own space.

RIYAD. I got my own space. My yard. Well, my mum's but
I got my own room, innit. I miss my Xbox, bruv.

CAIN. I'm PS4 all day, me.

RIYAD. *Gears of War*, fam. Back in the day, that was my shit.

CAIN. Yeah, that is a sick game, to be fair.

RIYAD. My Arsenal team on *FIFA* was sick. Kroos, Thomas Lemar, Harry Kane.

CAIN. As if. Harry Kane would never go Arsenal in a million years.

RIYAD. Why not?

CAIN. He's a yid.

RIYAD. He played for the Arsenal youth team.

CAIN. He never.

RIYAD. Swear down.

CAIN. He's overrated anyway. Should have signed Lewandowski. *I'm* better than Harry Kane.

RIYAD. Behave.

CAIN. Scored forty goals in one season for Netherley under-twelves. From the right wing.

RIYAD. I don't know what planet you live on, blud.

I fucking miss school, bruv. I didn't never think I'd say that.

CAIN. I got expelled from every school in the county. Mr Godfrey, he was my tutor in my last school before I went PRU. Said I was *unteachable*.

RIYAD. Thinking about it, school was the shit, innit? Footie at breaktimes with the mandem, all them gyal.

CAIN. Soon as I get out I'm gonna get my rod, get my bike…

RIYAD. I'm gonna get one of them VR sets for my Xbox, trust.

CAIN. Have a burger and chips from the van down Lee Park.

RIYAD. I bet bare sick new games have come out.

CAIN. Watch some proper porn. I'm gonna wank meself silly.

RIYAD. How's that different to now?

CAIN. *Actual* fucking porn, like.

You got any Black Jacks in that pack?

RIYAD. Yeah. I always ask the bredder on the counter to take
'em out, but –

CAIN. Swap yer.

RIYAD. You like 'em?

CAIN. Yeah.

RIYAD. For what?

CAIN. Depends. How many have you got?

RIYAD. Two, three... Five.

CAIN. I'll give you... one Dip Dab, *and* right... half of this –

RIYAD. I don't want half of nothing you've already bit into.

CAIN. I haven't bit into it, I broke it off –

RIYAD. Them's teeth marks, bruv.

CAIN. That's not teeth marks. It's just cus it's chewy.

RIYAD. How about a Dip Dab and some of them foamy
bananas –

CAIN. Two.

RIYAD. Four.

CAIN. No way, four!

RIYAD. Three.

CAIN. Two.

RIYAD. How about I take your bananas and give you nothing?

CAIN. Alright, I'll give yer a –

JONJO *enters again.*

RIYAD. Yo, man.

CAIN. Have you just been outside all the time?

JONJO. ,

RIYAD. Wagwan, blud?

JONJO. I used to w-walk my dog down to Hayes Street Farm
and cut across the common to Norman… Park. Sometimes
I'd walk her for hours. I'd throw her a stick and people
would… pet her and behind the cricket club was some water
she'd swim in if sh-she got h-h-hot. I'd just sit in the field.
When we moved to London I didn't even know you could…
that there were any fields to sit in.

That's where I met Jess. She had a Staffordshire terrier.

Usually by the time I got home the shouting would have
stopped. The door to their bedroom would be… closed. My
mum would be in the kitchen cooking or just looking out the
window. I always asked if she w-wanted to come and walk
with me. That w-we should go together. But she always said
no and that she had things to do.

I got back from school. It was Wednesday cus I had my PE
b-bag and there was crashing and shouting and… crying.
I got my dog lead and a new b-ball I'd gotten her for her…
birthday and I was trying to get her lead on while they were
arguing in the next room but she was upset my dog and
wouldn't sit still so I couldn't g-get her l-lead on. I was in
the kitchen a-a-and the back door was open ready to go and
just before I could get out the house my stepdad comes out
the living room and kicks her. My dog. T-twice. Just kicks
her b-because she's b-barking and upset b-by the noise.
I could hear M-Mum in the f-front room crying and…

They said I hit him with the kettle. Forty-eight times. I don't
really remember.

My dog is called M-Molly. Mum always forgets t-to feed her.

JONJO *exits*.

A beat.

RIYAD. Fucking told you, blud.

THREE

RIYAD, CAIN *and* JONJO *watch on as* GRACE *performs vigorous CPR on a baby doll.*

GRACE (*giving compressions*). You've really got to… be quite forceful… with the compressions… in order to have an impact.

CAIN. I dunno, man…

RIYAD. That's gonna hurt it.

GRACE. I'm not hurting the baby… (*Blows twice into the doll's mouth.*) And then back to compressions, okay?

You won't hurt it. But you do need to get the heart pumping again. So, it's two breaths and…

CAIN *and* RIYAD *shrug.*

JONJO. Th-thirty c-c…

CAIN. He's saying –

GRACE. Let him finish.

JONJO. C-c… compressions.

GRACE. Exactly. Thirty. It's very important you complete each cycle. Who wants to have another go?

CAIN. I saw Holly Willoughby doing this shit on *This Morning*. You could see right down her top, like.

RIYAD. Bruv. I'll compress that chest *all* day.

GRACE. Well volunteered, Riyad.

RIYAD. Shit.

RIYAD *self-consciously swaps positions with* GRACE.

Alright, cool, so…

GRACE. First of all, we…?

RIYAD. Like… blow in the mouth?

GRACE. Not quite. First is…

RIYAD. Shit, I dunno…

   RIYAD *looks for help*.

GRACE. Open the…

RIYAD. Open the mouth. Airway, thing. Open the airway.

GRACE. That's it. Great. Make sure it's not being blocked by anything. If it's clear you can just tilt the head back slightly, brilliant. And now…

RIYAD. I ain't putting my mouth where that dickhead's been slobbering all over it.

CAIN. Fuck right off, that weren't me.

RIYAD. He was putting his tongue in there and shit.

CAIN. As if, you meff.

GRACE. It's perfectly clean. That's what the wipes are for. So, five initial breaths, okay?

   RIYAD *hesitates – then lowers himself over the doll and blows weakly into its mouth*.

   Okay. Bit harder. We need the chest to inflate. So… yeah, bit harder.

CAIN. *Harder, harder.*

GRACE. Thank you, Cain.

RIYAD. It's not working.

GRACE. It will. Keep trying.

   RIYAD *blows harder*.

   That's it.

RIYAD. Yeah?

GRACE. Yeah, perfect.

RIYAD. Cool.

GRACE. So, five of those and then –

RIYAD. Do the compressions thing?

GRACE. That's right. Do you want to carry on?

RIYAD. Yeah, yeah.

GRACE. Okay, so two fingers, that's it. Now push down until you feel resistance.

RIYAD. Feels weird pushing down this hard, still.

GRACE. That's exactly it. Well done.

CAIN *has lost interest and is cradling a different doll.*

CAIN. What we doing this for, anyway? This is, like, advanced baby shit. What happened to feeding and nappies and that?

GRACE. Well, you were all doing so well and I thought...

RIYAD. The governor's on the wing, innit.

CAIN. Number one? Who told you that?

RIYAD. Bradley.

CAIN (*to* GRACE). That true, like?

GRACE. He might be popping in, maybe, I don't know. (*To* RIYAD.) So, now two more breaths and then carry on...

CAIN *chucks the baby doll at* JONJO, *who just about manages to catch it.*

CAIN. What's he doing down here?

JONJO. M-making sure we're okay?

CAIN. Like he gives a shit. As long as we're not tearing the place apart and he's getting paid his nice fat wedge, he couldn't give two fat fucks what happens to us.

RIYAD. I heard he got an MBE, yano. Like Jamal Edwards, innit. If they ever offered me a MBE or some shit I'd say fuck that. It's a fucking tool of the empire, innit. If you take one, you're condoning the violence on like India and Africa and shit.

GRACE (*indicating baby*). Riyad.

RIYAD. Sorry.

CAIN. What's MBE mean, anyway? Massive... Bell-end...

GRACE. It *means*, Member of the Order of the British Empire.

CAIN. Order of... what?

RIYAD. Basically, you're a snake, innit.

CAIN. Good job they ain't never gonna give you one then, eh?

RIYAD. Might do. I'm gonna do better things than that wasteman. I heard he's on like his third wife or whatever cus he keeps cheating on 'em and getting with some new younger bi...

Woman.

CAIN. That's horrid. Who'd marry him? He's a fat cunt.

GRACE. Cain!

RIYAD. And none of his kids speak to him no more.

CAIN. And he's telling me I'm the problem? Thinking he's better than me. I'm always gonna be a problem to people like him, innit. Nothing I ever do is right. Where I live is a problem, what music I listen to is a problem, what I wear is a problem. Whenever we have kids, it's a problem. Innit, Grace?

They should just fucking come clean and admit they just don't like us and that's why they locked us up in here.

JONJO. Didn't you b-beat up someone in a newsagent's?

CAIN. That's not the fucking point. What I'm saying is... is...

RIYAD. What?

CAIN. I'm making a point, aren't I? Fuck off. I dunno.

GRACE (*to* CAIN). Come and have a proper go at this, please.

CAIN. Do I have to?

GRACE. No, you don't have to.

CAIN. But you'll write it on my card, won't yer?

GRACE. I'll *have* to write it on the report, yes.

A fleeting stand-off that GRACE *wins.* RIYAD *and* CAIN *swap places.*

That was perfect, Riyad. Well done.

RIYAD. Safe, yeah. Cheers.

CAIN. Nobody better come in here and see me doing this.

If Ry Buckley even pokes his nose in here for a second I'm gonna jab my finger in his good eye. Stupid goggle-eyed twat.

JONJO. What's... wrong with it?

CAIN. I *dunno*? It just looks fucking weird. It gives me the creeps, know what I mean? Can't tell if he's looking at me or not.

JONJO. No. Why don't you w-w-want anyone to... see?

CAIN. Why?

RIYAD. Bruv, trust me.

CAIN. *Why?*

JONJO. Yeah.

CAIN. Everyone will laugh at us.

JONJO. So?

CAIN. *So...* everyone will laugh at us.

RIYAD. You do not want mans seeing this, trust.

CAIN. They'll all absolutely piss themselves. You'll never hear the end of it.

JONJO. They're a-all in lessons anyway.

CAIN. Yeah, normal lessons. Like learning how to be a sparky. Or a brickie. Not fucking changing nappies and how to make memories by teaching your stupid kid how to ride a bike. No one taught me how to ride a bike. Had to learn on me own.

I thought it'd be a doss.

GRACE. Well, I think Jonjo's right. There's nothing to be embarrassed about.

CAIN. You would say that.

GRACE. Ready to give it a go, then?

CAIN. *Yes*, alright. I'm doing it. What am I? Kunta Kinte?

RIYAD (*giving* CAIN *a playful slap*). Dickhead.

CAIN. Ah, you prick. Keep pushing. See what happens.

RIYAD. Yeah, whatever, man.

GRACE. Concentrate, please.

> GRACE *guides* CAIN *through the process.*

JONJO (*to* RIYAD). Could I do... history? Do they do stuff like that here?

RIYAD. Not generally, like. Depends, innit.

JONJO. On wh-what?

RIYAD. Whether they got anyone interested. You good at it, yeah?

> JONJO *nods.*

CAIN (*coming up for air*). What the fuck do you wanna do that for?

JONJO. I liked it... at school.

GRACE. Cain...

CAIN. Did you know something boring happened to someone really fucking ugly ages and ages ago? There you go. Here's your history GCSE.

No, wait. The king of wherever shagged some ugly bird from somewhere else and they had a war cus they were all bored off their tits cus there was no TV. So they sent all the peasants to get fucked up in a field and had a right good laugh about it. History.

Even bigger cunts than the governor, kings and queens, I'm telling yer.

GRACE. Your baby's not breathing.

CAIN. This baby's a headache.

GRACE. Compressions. Go. Now.

RIYAD (*to* JONJO). Might do, bruv. I heard up Hindley they got Pilates, still. Have to ask, innit. Jake'd know if they could sort it out for you.

JONJO. Right. Thanks.

Did you... make up with... your g-girlfriend?

RIYAD. Nah, fam. Not really. She ain't replying.

JONJO. Did your m-mum speak to her?

RIYAD. Didn't want to get involved, she said.

JONJO. Right.

RIYAD. She wasn't even right, yano? Serita. Jake let me go on one of the computers and I printed out all this shit to read about it and turns out Sagittarius and Pisces ain't no good like she said it was. So, if it is all real and shit, her and Jamz are fucked, anyway.

CAIN. I would honestly pay actual money for Akeem to come in here and see you blowing in a baby's mouth talking about star signs.

RIYAD. He wouldn't say shit. I run this ting in here, you just live here.

CAIN. *King Kong ain't got shit on me!*

You motherfuckers gonna be playing basketball in Pelican Bay when I get finished with you.

CAIN *looks expectantly at* GRACE.

GRACE. **,**

Training Day.

CAIN. Yes! *Finally.*

GRACE. I have seen some films.

RIYAD. That was pretty good, still. Denzel is my G.

JONJO. What's that?

RIYAD. *Bruv.*

CAIN. Did you grow up in a cupboard, like? Ain't you never seen *Training Day*? (*To* RIYAD.) *Mate*, you seen *The Equalizer*? Sick film. The lads got, like this mad Robert Downey Jr. Sherlock Holmes shit where he can imagine the fight before –

GRACE. Okay, okay. Enough. *Enough*. Carry on.

CAIN (*about* JONJO). Why can't he do it?

JONJO. Do your… you know… do they ever come to visit?

RIYAD. Kids?

JONJO *nods*.

CAIN. Not me, la. He'll be in here himself soon enough, like.

RIYAD. Me either, man. I ain't on good terms right now but, yano… I wouldn't let him anyway. It's weird. They like screen 'em, innit? Check inside their shoes for shit and make them open their mouths. Make sure they ain't bringing nothing inside. Drugs and blades and shit. I'm talking, like… one-, two-year-olds, fam. I had to do that when I was little. To go and see my dad. Like… that shouldn't be a normal thing for a little kid to do, still?

JONJO. Right. Yeah.

GRACE. Shall we leave it there for today?

The doll, Cain? Thank you.

CAIN *passes the doll*.

RIYAD *picks up a letter lying on the ground*.

That was good, today. I know that was a bit of a leap but it's an important one. You all did really well.

CAIN. What we doing next week?

GRACE. What would you like to do?

CAIN. Oh, whatever? I dunno.

GRACE. We could try feeding again? Or…

CAIN. They're doing footie trials next week, so I might not be here, anyway. So, you know, do whatever.

GRACE (*to* RIYAD *and* JONJO). Should I plan for your absences as well? More budding athletes?

RIYAD. Nah, man. I'll be here, innit.

JONJO. D-did you ever have to do that, miss?

GRACE. Do what? Oh. No. Thankfully. But, you know, I've definitely had my moments.

CAIN. Like what?

GRACE. Well… There was the time I had to take Alex to the hospital to have his head glued. That was pretty scary. And when he broke his arm skateboarding. And then when he broke it again. Skateboarding.

RIYAD. Rah, you might want to keep an eye on your kid, innit, Grace.

GRACE. Thanks for the advice, Riyad. I'll bear it in mind.

It happens. You know that's… life. That's kids. You can't watch them every second of every day. They bump their heads and graze their knees and… come to you to make it better. And that's what you have to do.

I'll see you next week, okay? I know Mr Harris didn't end up coming in but, I think, if he had, he'd be really impressed. Someone will be along to pick you up in a minute. Have a good week.

GRACE *exits*.

CAIN. Give it. Just give it here.

RIYAD. What?

CAIN. You fucking know what. It's not in my pocket. Give it.

RIYAD (*holding the letter*). This?

CAIN. Yes. Give it here.

RIYAD. Well, I don't want to know.

CAIN. Why not?

RIYAD. Cus you're getting all aggy. Blatantly don't want me to see it, which makes me wanna look at it.

CAIN. Give me my fucking letter.

CAIN *reaches out,* RIYAD *pulls it away.*

RIYAD. What is it?

CAIN. It's nothing. It's mine. Give it here.

RIYAD. I was, but now I think I should give it a proper read, still.

CAIN. I said it give it.

RIYAD *fends off* CAIN *as he opens the letter.*

RIYAD. Whoa, you've read this bare, innit. Dear Mr Walters… yeah, yeah… We are writing to you –

CAIN. Fuck off, you cunt. La, la, la, la.

(*To* JONJO.) Don't listen or I'll fucking batter yer.

JONJO. Don't f-fight.

RIYAD. Writing to you to follow up on… yeah, yeah, yeah… What you getting so aggy for? Calm, bruv.

CAIN. It's my letter.

RIYAD. Yeah, and I'm fucking reading it. Didn't your mum never tell you it's rude to snatch.

CAIN. No, she never. Give it.

RIYAD. It was on the floor.

CAIN (*pulling sweets out*). Just give it back and you can have these. Whatever you want. Dip Dabs, bananas, whatever.

RIYAD. We hope you have given due consideration –

CAIN. I'm gonna fucking nut you, I swear.

RIYAD. Offer you the chance to speak to Mr Alexandre… Alexandrescu? Fuck me, where's he from… Face to face… the meeting will be arranged under supervision… process called restorative… justice?

CAIN *finally snatches the letter.*

Bruv.

CAIN. Thanks a fucking lot.

RIYAD. Bro.

CAIN. What? What you looking at me like that for?

RIYAD. This means what I think it does, yeah?

CAIN. I dunno what you think, do I?

RIYAD. What ya hiding that for? That's sick, man.

CAIN. I was hiding it because it's none of your fucking business, you nosy dickhead.

JONJO. What's sick?

RIYAD. You wanna tell him?

CAIN. I didn't *wanna* tell you.

JONJO. What is it?

RIYAD. Basically, yeah… it's a letter saying if he goes and links the bre he fucked up and they have like… some meetings and shit and talk about what happened, he'll get a recommendation towards his sentence so he could do the rest outside on tag or whatever.

JONJO. That's good.

CAIN. Yeah, great. Whoop-de-fucking-doo.

RIYAD. Don't be a waste about it, man. (*To* JONJO.) It is.

CAIN. No, it isn't.

RIYAD. What's wrong with it?

CAIN. Fucking apologise to him and look like a twat. As fucking if.

RIYAD. Why not?

CAIN. Cus I'll look a right dickhead.

RIYAD. So what? Ain't no one gonna know except you and him.

CAIN. And you, now.

RIYAD. Bruv, I ain't gonna tell no one.

CAIN. I'm not fucking apologising to him. He's a dickhead. He deserved what he got. If I could go back I'd do it again.

Fucking following me round every day like I'm gonna rob the shop!

RIYAD. Don't be stupid, blud.

CAIN. Don't call me stupid. I'm not stupid.

RIYAD. You probably ain't even gotta say sorry, man. Just like... recognise what you done wasn't the best course of action or whatever they want you to say. Who cares what you gotta say, anyway? You got a chance to duck out of here whenever you want. That's a fucking winning lottery ticket, blud.

How long you had that for?

CAIN. I dunno. Few weeks.

RIYAD. A few *weeks*? Fam.

CAIN. So what?

RIYAD. And you ain't done nothing about it?

CAIN. No.

RIYAD. You could go and see your kid. All this stuff we been doing here. What you been doing it for if you're just gonna stay in here?

CAIN. Why the fuck are any of us here? Why the fuck is *he* doing any of it? His kid's gonna be older than us by the time he gets out of here after what he done. What the fuck's he learning to change nappies for?

RIYAD. Don't be a dickhead.

CAIN. What? It's the fucking truth.

RIYAD. He ain't done nothing to you. Don't take your shit out on him.

CAIN. We're just pretending. Getting through the fucking day. Like we'd ever be fucking good dads.

RIYAD. I'm gonna be.

CAIN. Yeah, fucking, course you will, lad. Yeah.

RIYAD. It gets you out of here. That's it, blud. Bottom line, you get to *go*, innit. Finish early. Think of all the man that would

kill for that piece of fucking paper. You gonna be like
Johnny, yeah? Too scared to fucking leave.

CAIN. Yeah, why don't you do it, then? If you wanna do it so
much?

RIYAD. They ain't offering it to me.

JONJO. Wh-why don't you –

CAIN. Shut up, yer prick!

RIYAD. *Don't* tell him to shut up.

CAIN. Yeah, what you gonna do? Walking round here like the
big fucking 'I am'. Telling me what to do.

(*Starts to rip the letter.*) Fuck the letter. And fuck him. And
fuck you!

RIYAD *rushes* CAIN. *Grabs him by the collar. Slams him
against the wall.*

RIYAD. You don't use that to get out of here, blud, I'll fucking
kill you. No joke. I will fucking kill you. One way or another
you're out of here. You get me?

CAIN. Fucking go on, then. Get out of here, yeah? Go back
home?

What fucking home? I ain't got one. I don't know what that
word means. This place here… is like fucking Butlin's to
me. It's like a holiday compared to where I'm from. You
think I wanna go back there? That fucking shithole. I ain't
got no family, I ain't got nowhere to live, no money. What
am I leaving for? This is *it*.

Happy, yeah? Now I've said it? Fucking… prick.

Get the fuck off me.

CAIN *wrestles free of* RIYAD's *grasp*.

CAIN *exits*.

RIYAD *boots one of the chairs – narrowly missing* JONJO.

RIYAD. Fuck.

JONJO. Are you alright?

RIYAD. Yeah, I'm fucking cool. Yeah. Just…

Give me a minute.

RIYAD *paces – calming himself.*

Don't listen to him, man. You know… what he said. He don't know shit.

JONJO. I… It's okay.

RIYAD. Nah, it ain't. He shouldn't be saying that.

JONJO. It's true.

RIYAD. Don't matter.

RIYAD *picks up the two torn pieces of the letter.*

JONJO. What are you going to do?

RIYAD. Give him the letter.

JONJO. He said he doesn't want to do it.

RIYAD. He don't know what he wants.

JONJO. S-seemed pretty sure.

RIYAD. Wouldn't you do it? If you could? If they offered it to you?

JONJO. No one to apologise to.

RIYAD. Nah. You sorted that, for real.

If he don't do this, he'll regret it, trust. Come, back me. He might listen to you.

JONJO. Me?

RIYAD. I dunno. Worth a try, innit. Come.

(*Exiting through the door.*) Oi, bruv. You still there?

RIYAD *exits.*

JONJO *exits.*

FOUR

RIYAD *and* JONJO *are playing Connect 4. Mouse Trap sits half-finished on another table.*

RIYAD*'s foot is in a protective shoe.*

RIYAD. Mans thinking they're big cus they throwing a few chairs in the canteen. Wait till they get moved up, innit.

JONJO. Is it a lot… worse?

RIYAD. Just different. Some of the olders told me they actually preferred it to coming here. Get to wear your own garms, innit. But it's definitely more serious. You get beef with the wrong bredder in proper pen you gonna end up done, you get me? In here it's all these pussy'oles pretending like they're somebody, chatting bare shit. Just trying to get themselves a rep, innit.

Your turn.

JONJO. I'm thinking.

RIYAD. Bruv, it's Connect 4, not fucking Chess.

JONJO. Don't rush me.

RIYAD. Look, I'm just saying mans got things to do and I can't be held back from realising my potential cus they keep banging us up. I missed two classes cus of that shit.

JONJO. There.

RIYAD. Finally. And… *boom*. That's how it's done.

Did you find out if they're gonna let you take that history thing you wanted to do?

JONJO. They said I… couldn't sign up until my case has been p-processed.

RIYAD. So, how comes you're in here doing the childcare ting?

JONJO. They had space.

RIYAD. When I got sent down I said not guilty at first, innit. Not guilty, not guilty. And then when it comes to trial I stand up and I'm like, yeah, mate, guilty. The look on his face. They said, why'd you say not guilty at your pre-hearing if you were just going to change your plea? And I said cus this girl is pregnant with my baby, and I wanted to meet him before I go away, you get me? And I got to. Once. Before coming in here. And they was pissed off, man. But it was worth it. Seeing that little kid.

They let you listen on the phone if you're in here when it happens, still. But that wasn't enough for me.

JONJO. They let you listen?

RIYAD. Yeah. Better than nothing. Ring up the hospital and some nurse or whatever is on the end telling you wagwan. Get to talk to your girl and that, tell her it's all good.

JONJO. They wouldn't let me talk to her. Her parents.

RIYAD. They might stop you talking to her but can't stop you being on the phone, innit. That's your kid, not theirs. You wanna listen, at least. Screaming and all that, yeah. But when you hear it. For the first time. Fam. I tell you.

JONJO. What?

RIYAD. Those little lungs. First sounds. Crying out for you. Tell you, G. I almost dropped the ting. Mad experience. Worth the extra few months they gave me for wasting time, innit.

Wait… when did you? How'd you keep doing this?

RIYAD *brushes his remaining counters away.*

JONJO. Want to play something else?

RIYAD. He's taking his time, innit?

JONJO. Maybe he went back to his pad?

RIYAD. Check you with the lingo. Doubt it. I ain't never seen him stay in there 'less he gets made to, innit. And he's been shut up in there for long.

Your mum come visit you, yet?

JONJO *shakes his head.*

Write to you?

JONJO. She's on her own now.

RIYAD. Thought you had a little sister?

JONJO. She's at my… my…

RIYAD *waits*.

G-grandparents. She's only seven.

RIYAD. Yeah? Shit.

My mums never came at first. Wouldn't talk to me. Stopped my little brother talking to me. They're the only people I got and they were just… gone. I guess she just needed time, innit. Time to, like, be angry at me.

It was hard, still. Felt proper guilty, innit. And then I was angry cus I was on road cus of her, sort of. She wasn't never there. We didn't have no money. So I thought I didn't have no choice. And I just… then I was angry at her, for being angry at me and… it was this whole headfuck, man. But we're cool now. She knows I'm doing my classes and… she comes visit. I can still see she's like worried, yano… like, that won't ever go, that worrying. Not now. Just in case I do something to fuck it up again, you get me?

Your mum might come, still, is what I'm saying.

CAIN *enters*.

CAIN. Alright, dickheads?

RIYAD. You was in there long.

CAIN. What happened? Don't tell me you already told him, I jibbed that meeting off fast as I could, like.

RIYAD. Maybe you should have took it serious, innit.

CAIN. *Sorry*, Mum.

RIYAD. What happened to footie trials?

CAIN. What are you? My fucking PA? Didn't fancy it, did I? Thought I'd give the others a chance, like.

RIYAD. Sure, bruv.

CAIN. They kept me in my cell three fucking days straight cus of Johnny Corbett. That kid is a straight-up weapon. I'm trying to eat my scran and there's fucking chairs flying over me head. He's lost it. Should have kept him in the ozzy. He's not right up here.

RIYAD. That's what I'm saying.

CAIN. So, go 'ed. What happened?

RIYAD. What you on about?

CAIN. What do you think? Your fucking foot, la. I heard it all from Ry but he's a lying little cunt and I told him we did classes together. That shut him right up.

RIYAD. Nothing to tell.

CAIN. So, you go schitzo at me and then three days later –

RIYAD. I said sorry, didn't I?

CAIN. *Three days* later I hear you and Akeem are scrapping? Latest fashion, is it? We all getting one?

RIYAD. Just a hairline fracture, still.

JONJO. Does anyone want to play Mouse Trap?

CAIN. Mouse Trap is for queers.

JONJO. I think she said there's… Battleships.

CAIN. I heard he got in your pad? Ry said he's been planning it for months.

RIYAD. Nothing happened.

CAIN. You should fucking do him. He's got it coming, he's always chatting shit.

RIYAD. Don't start.

CAIN. So what? You fell out of bed? Tripped down the stairs?

RIYAD. Exactly. (*To* JONJO.) Get Battleships out, then. I gotta beat you at something, this is getting embarrassing…

CAIN (*shadow-boxing*). I heard you got some good digs in, like.

RIYAD. I don't know what the fuck you're talking about.

JONJO. I think it's missing some parts.

CAIN. I think *you're* missing some parts.

(*To* RIYAD.) You're telling me that it's just a coincidence that there's a big fucking scrap in the canteen and neither you nor Akeem was there and two days after you're walking around with a fucking space boot on yer foot –

RIYAD. It's not broken. It's fractured. It's the metatarsal. I got it playing footie, innit, and I wasn't there cus I wasn't hungry.

CAIN. How did he get in there? Don't they usually keep you apart cus of all the… fucking… gang shit?

RIYAD. Bruv. Allow it. Don't say *gang* in here, man. Get me back on D-wing.

CAIN. I won't say nothing. (*To* JONJO.) You won't say nothing, will yer?

RIYAD. There ain't nothing *to* say.

CAIN. Everyone knows it fucking happened even if neither of you are saying shi–

RIYAD. Will you just let a man play fucking Battleships? Fuck! I'm not about that any more.

I didn't touch Akeem. Akeem didn't come nowhere near me. I don't want to fucking *think* about Akeem. Man wanna play Battleships, do my meeting, go back to my yard and study for my non-calculator test.

B-five.

JONJO. Miss.

RIYAD. Shit.

CAIN, *circling*.

CAIN. Hurry your meeting up, eh? We're doing feeding after. I been practising.

JONJO. Practising?

CAIN. Yeah.

RIYAD. You been practising?

CAIN. *Yeah*.

RIYAD. How do you practise that? What with?

CAIN. A Capri-Sun. I'm getting good at it.

RIYAD. Why you been practising for?

CAIN. Dunno! I was bored. Fuck.

Has she brought anything decent? Game of Life? What the fuck is that?

JONJO. It's where you get a job. And have kids and go on h-holiday. Things like that.

CAIN. Why would I wanna play a game where I have to get a job?

RIYAD. Says the dickhead practising how to feed a baby.

F-six.

JONJO. Sorry, no.

CAIN. How's that different to you doing maths in your room?

RIYAD. Cus that's actually gonna get me somewhere.

CAIN. Sitting in a room doing sums on a calculator for the rest of your life.

RIYAD. Better than being in here.

JONJO. Probably get paid well.

RIYAD. Exactly. Gonna make that big pea.

CAIN. Easier ways to make a fat wedge. You gonna go to work every day for eight hours a day for... forty years? That's madness.

RIYAD. Nah, bruv. Staying in here talking to you every day would be a madness. I'd go fucking insane.

JONJO. H-ten.

RIYAD. Are you like the Mr Miyagi of board games or something? Hit.

(*To* CAIN.) I'm gonna start my own business. Take care of my kid. I'm gonna decide what I do for a fucking change. I'm being the me I should have been. And you'll fucking wish you listened to me, innit.

CAIN. *I look like you wanna look, I fuck like you wanna fuck, I am smart, capable and most importantly, I am free, in all the ways you are not.*

Right? No? *Fight Club.* Brad Pitt? I'm fucking wasted on you lot, that was spot-on.

RIYAD. You're a waste, full stop. (*To* JONJO.) A-nine.

JONJO. Miss.

The door opens and GRACE *leans in.*

GRACE. When you're ready, Riyad.

RIYAD *looks round and* GRACE *taps her watch.* GRACE *exits.*

CAIN. Oh yeah, she said to go in.

RIYAD. And you didn't think to say nothing, yeah?

CAIN. *Sorry.* I forgot.

RIYAD. She's gonna think I was ignoring her, innit.

CAIN. So what?

RIYAD. I got revision to do, yano.

RIYAD *exits.*

CAIN. He thinks he's better than all of us in here. Just cus he can add a few numbers together. How hard can it be?

JONJO. What's six times seven?

CAIN. Forty... fuck you. How about that?

I should tell 'em I saw him and Akeem scrapping and get him locked up for another six months. Stick him back on basic. Take his GCSE away. That'd learn him. Wipe the smug smile off his face.

JONJO. You... wouldn't.

CAIN. I might. I'm unpredictable. That's what it says on my psych report. 'Problems with boundaries.'

How'd you play this, then?

JONJO. Battleships?

CAIN. Yeah, whatever it's called.

JONJO. You've never played Battleships?

CAIN. No. I was out. Doing other shit. Not being a fucking nerd playing board games.

JONJO. You put the ships here, in different places…

CAIN. So, what happened to your old fella, then?

JONJO. What? I thought you w-wanted to play Battleships?

CAIN. Nah.

JONJO. Why do you wanna know?

CAIN. It's what she's gonna try and get out of yer in there. You could swerve it, like, but…

JONJO. I told you what happened.

CAIN. Not that divvy. Yer real one.

JONJO. D-don't… don't know. Left, I spose.

CAIN. Just fucking left, like?

JONJO. I was little. Don't really remember him.

CAIN. Nah. Me neither, like.

JONJO. ,

CAIN. He come to visit me, once. I had no fucking idea who he was, like. But he got visitation and they take me in the meeting room where people meet, like, foster parents and that and he turns up with this Arctic roll, from Iceland. I was six. It was my birthday. Never seen him in my life but I could see I looked like him, even then. We sat there and didn't really chat nor nothing, just ate this Arctic roll which he hadn't even defrosted properly. Still frozen in the middle. Useless fucking meff.

Topped himself. Apparently. Fucking glad cus he sounds like a prick. I was a little kid living with random fucking strangers that cared more about me than he did. Or they was paid to care, anyway. You've got to be some sort of prick to do that to yourself when you've got a little kid, haven't yer?

JONJO. Yeah.

CAIN. Or just not right in the head. And you don't want someone for a dad who's not right in the head, do yer? Better off without him.

JONJO. Are you... okay.

CAIN. Yeah. Why?

JONJO. You seem a bit...

CAIN. Hectic, like?

JONJO. Yeah.

CAIN. Too much time on me own. You know how it is. Get a bit fucking cooped up, like. Head goes a bit weird. Glad to be here, to be honest.

It's Johnny, like, tell you the truth. He's put me right on edge. He's a poof, like, and obviously I'd have him in a fair fight but he's in the pad next to mine, right? And he's gone. Like... I mean, *gone*. Switched, like. Who knows what the fuck he's gonna do next, know what I mean? Gives me the 'eebie-jeebies. That's what my nan called 'em.

JONJO. Maybe you should tell someone?

CAIN. And say what? Can you take him somewhere else? We fucking *are* somewhere else. We are where people get taken. Nah, gonna have to sort it myself.

Go 'ed, then. Let's fucking set this Battleships up for when Riyad gets back.

JONJO. It's two-player.

CAIN. Oh. Well. Got to be something we can all three of us do, yeah? In this pile?

CAIN *rifling through the board games.*

What about this one?

JONJO. That's four.

CAIN. We ain't got four.

JONJO. Up to four.

CAIN (*sitting down to set up*). So, three, then? Why didn't you just say that. You're gonna have to show me what bit goes where, la.

JONJO *and* CAIN *set up the game.*

JONJO. At least he remembered your birthday.

CAIN. What?

JONJO. Your dad. When he came w-w-with the Arctic roll.

CAIN. Oh. Yeah. Spose he did, yeah.

FIVE

RIYAD *and* GRACE *are in a one-to-one session.*

RIYAD *is looking at a college prospectus.*

GRACE. So, what do you think?

RIYAD. I dunno. Yeah, I mean… I dunno.

GRACE. They've got really good facilities. You wouldn't just have to do Maths. There's Computer Science, or Economics…

RIYAD. Economics?

GRACE. You would have to take a couple of GCSEs as well, alongside your A levels. English and Science. Depends on their entry requirements.

RIYAD. What, I can't just do the Maths, nah?

GRACE. They do like you to have English and Science.

RIYAD. I wasn't no good at English at school.

GRACE. Well. You'd only need to get a C in your first year, or a five now, sorry. Then once you've got that, you can do whatever you want.

RIYAD (*reading*). What's Further Mathematics mean?

GRACE. Sorry?

RIYAD. What's Further Mathematics?

GRACE. Where does it say that?

RIYAD. Here. It says Mathematics and then on the next page it's Further Mathematics. That for the proper smart people, innit?

GRACE. Um, I don't think so. They probably just cover different topics.

A lapse. RIYAD, *uncomfortable.*

What is it?

RIYAD. What?

GRACE. What's up?

RIYAD. Nothing.

GRACE. Sure?

RIYAD. ,

GRACE. I thought you wanted to do this?

RIYAD. Nah, I do, still. Just… you know…

GRACE. Just?

RIYAD. Like, Further Mathematics, what the fuck is that? No one said nothing about that.

GRACE. Don't worry about that. We can go through that with you. You're clever enough to go, if that's what you're worrying about. You're absolutely clever enough to go.

RIYAD. How would you know that?

GRACE. Because I've taught you.

RIYAD. Not this shit.

GRACE. Jake showed me some of the work you've been doing.

RIYAD. My maths work?

GRACE. Yeah.

RIYAD. Did he tell you to do this?

GRACE. No.

RIYAD. Show me this thing?

GRACE. No. I brought this in. I thought you'd like it.

Don't they look like you? There. Couldn't you imagine that being you?

RIYAD. They're Asian. And they're *girls*.

GRACE (*smiling*). No, I just mean in the photo. What they're doing. I'm asking why couldn't that be you after you leave here?

RIYAD. What's funny?

GRACE. No, I was just… There's nothing funny about that. That's what I'm saying.

RIYAD. That ain't me.

GRACE. It could be. Why not?

RIYAD. Cus they ain't gonna want me, Grace. These people in here. Trust. Look at 'em. These other students ain't gonna want someone like me in their classes. Them teachers definitely won't.

RIYAD *closes the prospectus and discards it on the table.*

GRACE. I think you're wrong about that, Riyad. I think they'd be lucky to have you. This moment in your life, this place here, doesn't have to define you. Doesn't have to define your life.

RIYAD. Does Alex go uni or whatever?

GRACE. How old do you think I am?

RIYAD. Oh, I dunno... like...

GRACE. Be careful when you answer.

RIYAD *smiles, begrudgingly.*

He's not old enough yet. He might not go. He hasn't exactly excelled at school. We'll see.

RIYAD. Do they do what you do? For a A level.

GRACE. What I do?

RIYAD. The baby shit. All this you been teaching us.

GRACE. Not as an A level. It's probably one small module of part of a BTEC, or something. Unfortunately, skills like these are often overlooked.

RIYAD. Yeah, innit. They never taught me no useful shit at school. Like, how'd you get a flat or whatever? Or vote and shit like that? I ain't got a clue, man. They should teach you that stuff in case you ain't got no one to show you.

You should do this as an A level, innit.

GRACE. Thanks. So, what happened to your leg?

RIYAD. Nothing. It's cool. Door slammed on it.

GRACE. Right.

RIYAD. Don't hurt or nothing.

GRACE. That's good. How are you getting on with your non-calculator exam?

RIYAD. Yeah, it's calm.

GRACE. It's calm? Okay.

RIYAD. I'm doing past papers, innit.

GRACE. Past papers. I know them well.

And how are you feeling about seeing Marcus when you leave?

RIYAD. Marcus?

GRACE. Yeah.

RIYAD. I don't even know, yano. His mum's got loads of pictures of me on her phone, to show him, so he don't forget but... He'll look different, innit. My little boy. When I get out next year. Like... to the picture I've got in my head. Be like meeting him all over again. A whole new start.

GRACE. You'll have all the time in the world soon.

RIYAD. Yeah...

Yeah, man.

GRACE *holds out the prospectus for* RIYAD *to take.*

GRACE. Listen. No one's saying you have to go right now. Just think about it. Give it another look.

RIYAD. Did you give them man in there one of these? When you was chatting to 'em.

GRACE. No.

A beat before RIYAD *takes it.*

RIYAD. Cool.

RIYAD *exits.*

SIX

CAIN *and* JONJO *are play-boxing.*

JONJO *has a new pair of shoes on. They are the same as* RIYAD*'s.*

RIYAD *is struggling with a nappy.*

CAIN. They wanted me to move up a weight, like, cus no one my age could touch me. I was in the ring with older lads, right, when I was fourteen, just sparring, like, but they wanted to send me to the Junior World Championships. In Russia or Bulgaria or something they were but that's when I got sent to Parva.

No one could touch me. Too quick, right?

Jab, jab. Go 'ed.

JONJO *slowly follows his instruction.*

Five, left, five right. Come on, quicker than that.

RIYAD. I don't get this.

CAIN. They said I'd probably have been able to go pro if I'd wanted to. Like AJ or summat, bring out my own clothing range. The Hurri-Cain! Eh? Come on. Riyad, you could be my accountant. Sort out me taxes.

RIYAD. Yeah, let me think about that.

CAIN (*to* JONJO). Come on.

My nan could punch harder than that. You're lucky everyone is caking their pants cus of what you done. And you're a massive fucking tree.

JONJO. What did I do?

CAIN. You know… went all fucking…

CAIN *mimes* Psycho *dagger.*

I told 'em. Everyone thought you was a spastic and Ry was gonna jump you on social but I told him what you did and now he doesn't think he's so fucking hard. You're welcome, by the way.

Now try and hit me. Bet I'm too quick for yer. Try a hook, go on. Yeah, yeah.

JONJO *connects with a sharp, stinging punch.*

Ah, fuck! Agh. Yeah… right. Just… give us a second. Better, yeah.

JONJO. Are you okay?

CAIN. Oh, nah, yeah… Just caught me by surprise. Sound. You ever done this before?

JONJO. No.

CAIN. You might want to look into it.

RIYAD. I reckon this one's broken, innit.

CAIN. What's the matter, Rain Man? Too hard for yer?

RIYAD. These things is bad for the environment or some shit, anyway.

CAIN. Yeah, that's why you don't wanna use it, cus you care about the rainforests.

RIYAD. How'd you do it, then?

CAIN. Do I have to show everybody how to do everything? Here…

So, this goes under, right? Ah, this fucking hurts, Jonj, you prick… And you just use this tab here to tighten it. Piece of piss, la.

What?

RIYAD. I'm shocked. That's what.

CAIN. Cheers.

RIYAD. When did you learn to do that?

CAIN. We did these when you was off doing your fancy Maths exams. (*To* JONJO.) Didn't we?

JONJO. Yeah.

CAIN. How can you do all them sums but you can't even do up some Pampers?

RIYAD. How do you know they are Pampers when you can't even read the packet?

CAIN. If you're gonna be a cunt then I won't help yer. And Jake said I'm probably dyslexic so fuck you.

RIYAD. You're not dyslexic. Jake said that?

CAIN. Yer not the only one having one-on-ones, you know.

RIYAD. Said you was dyslexic?

CAIN. Yeah.

RIYAD. This like when people say they've got ADHD but actually they're just annoying little dickheads.

CAIN. Eh, maybe I've got that as well. What's it stand for? He said I could get tested.

RIYAD. They ain't got a test for whatever you are, trust.

CAIN. It's alright, I'm not trying to get in there with yer little bum-boy.

RIYAD. You said you didn't want him near you, anyway.

CAIN. I don't! But… you know, he was helping me with something.

RIYAD. Helping you? With what?

CAIN. They've decided I'm too dangerous to be in here with you muppets so they're starring me up and moving me straight to Belmarsh.

RIYAD. Course, fam, yeah. Ashfield, more like.

CAIN. Serious. They said I was the most dangerous prisoner since Bronson or summat.

RIYAD. Since Operation Yewtree.

CAIN. Joke's on you, cus I don't know what that is.

RIYAD. Do you know what he's talking about?

JONJO *nods*.

Oh, cool, yeah. Thanks very much.

CAIN. Didn't know you cared.

RIYAD. Come on, bruv, I told you 'bout that college thing.

CAIN. Oh, yeah, showing off, very noble of you, la.

RIYAD. Nah, it weren't like that. I told you cus –

CAIN. Alright! I'm just, like… you know, thought I'd give that thing a try. That letter I got sent.

RIYAD. Letter? What let– Oh! The letter. Shit. For real?

CAIN. Yeah, well. You made a big fucking deal out of it, didn't yer? Thought I'd better give it a go before you have a fucking stroke.

RIYAD. Shit.

CAIN. Yeah.

Just got to fucking… hear from him. He might not want to do it after all. Dunno. Might have changed his mind. But wrote the letter and that saying yeah, I wanna do it. If he says sound then I transfer somewhere closer and… see.

Sent it last week.

RIYAD. Right.

CAIN. Yeah.

RIYAD. How come?

CAIN. I dunno. Summat to do, like. I just thought… fuck it, you know?

RIYAD. Exactly. What you gotta lose?

You gonna see your…

CAIN. Might do? Yeah. Maybe? I dunno. I won't lie, I have thought about it. Maybe Shannon will be impressed I can do nappies and that and actually let me stay in her flat. Probably not, but you never know.

RIYAD. That'd be cool.

CAIN. Yeah. You two are gonna be fucking bawling when I go, aren't yer?

RIYAD. Fuck off, man. Counting down the days, innit. You just tell me the day you're leaving and I bet I can get all the mandem on the wing to give you some going-away beats.

CAIN. I'll just slip away, mate. Everyone will be like… where's Cain gone? I'll become a myth, a legend. I'm already a legend, to be fair. This'll just add to it.

RIYAD. Bruv, we'll forget you in a minute.

CAIN. Oh yeah, I forgot about all yer other mates you'll be hanging around with.

RIYAD. We are not… We don't *hang out*. I have to come here.

CAIN. You don't have to come here. (*Going to the door.*) Maybe they'll get the new lads in here. Get yourself a new maths buddy? You can wank each other off to the periodic table.

RIYAD. That's chemistry, you dickhead.

CAIN. Alright, fucking… *sums*, then. Multiplication tables. Whatever.

RIYAD. What d'you say?

CAIN. I said, you can wank each other off over multiplicat–

RIYAD. There's new mans on the wing?

CAIN. Oh. Two new lads, yeah.

Came in yesterday. They was in Jake's office getting sorted this morning. I seen the mixed-race one before and Zahid says he was at Cookham with him. Don't know the other one, apparently called Ibby.

I thought maybe we'd get sneaky peek at them coming out, getting shown round and that. (*To* JONJO.) Either of 'em on two?

JONJO *shakes his head.*

RIYAD *pushes* CAIN *out the way of the door.*

They're not there now. I told yer. Probably padded up before scran time.

RIYAD. Ibby, yeah? What he look like?

CAIN. I dunno. I only saw the back of his head. He did look hard, like.

RIYAD. How could you possibly tell that?

CAIN. Just… looked it. You know… how he was walking and that. I'm not saying I couldn't have him, like. Obviously. He just looked… serious.

RIYAD. Serious?

CAIN. Yeah.

RIYAD. You can't tell that from the back of some man's head.

CAIN. Course you can. (*To* JONJO.) Turn around, big man.

RIYAD (*to* JONJO). Don't turn around.

CAIN. Now if he doesn't turn around he's just doing what you told him to do. Just turn around.

RIYAD. Don't turn around.

CAIN. Nah, come on, look, just to prove me point, like.

RIYAD. Don't do what he tells ya.

CAIN. You're gonna break him. Look how confused he is.

RIYAD. He's not a dog.

CAIN (*manoeuvring* JONJO). He don't mind. You don't mind, do yer?

RIYAD. Fine, blud. Whatever. Turn around. Do a little dance if he asks you to, innit.

CAIN *and* RIYAD *survey the back of* JONJO's *head*.

CAIN. See? Tell me you can't tell he looks like a spaz. And definitely not hard.

JONJO. H-hey!

RIYAD (*laughing*). What a dickhead, man.

CAIN *starts to shadow-box around* JONJO.

CAIN. He knows I'm only joking. I'm just trying to toughen him up, like. So he doesn't fall apart once I've gone. When I'm not here to protect him and look out for his fat arse.

JONJO *cuffs* CAIN, *or pushes him – either way he goes a distance.*

Shit. Ow, man.

Maybe I've taught you enough.

JONJO *offers to help him back to his feet.*

CAIN *scrambles up on his own.*

(*To* RIYAD.) Why'd you care, anyway? Not expecting anyone, are yer?

RIYAD. Nah. I'm cool.

CAIN. Scared?

RIYAD. No.

CAIN. I thought you was all reformed and shit, anyway.

RIYAD. I said I'm cool.

JONJO. You won't get to finish the course.

CAIN. Can't be that much left to do. I mean, they're only kids, aren't they? Fuck. Don't drop it. If it cries it wants feeding.

Or burping.

JONJO. Or needs changing.

CAIN. Right. Play with it. Don't leave it alone. Don't give it booze or let it smoke ciggies and definitely don't let it have a cheeky line just to see what happens, she did make that very clear.

JONJO. Bath it.

CAIN. Oh yeah, important, that. Clean it. Talc it. Hmm.

Don't give it loads of sweets. Rots yer teeth.

JONJO. Sing to it?

CAIN. Alright, Freddie Mercury.

JONJO. Like nursery rhymes and stuff.

CAIN. Yeah, well, nursery rhymes, that's fair enough, that.

JONJO. Read to it?

CAIN. Might have to get Shannon to do that bit.

RIYAD. That's just babies though, innit. What about when it gets walking? Or like teenagers and shit? She ain't said nothing about when they get older.

CAIN. That's ages away.

RIYAD. Yeah?

CAIN. Yeah. Years. By then everyone's just making it up as they go along.

I'll just tell him. Don't be like me. Best advice I could give yer. See what I do? Don't do that and what I don't do, do that. See?

RIYAD. Oh yeah. Simple. Why didn't I think of that?

They sit in silence for a while, pondering.

CAIN. Wait... have you two got the same trainees? He's gone and bought your fucking trabs!

JONJO. I... I...

CAIN. What are you? Fucking bezzie... shoe... mates?

RIYAD. Yeah, good one.

JONJO. I don't know how that happened...

CAIN. I fucking do. Basically, what you've done is he's got the trainees and then you've saved up and bought the trainees that's he's got, that's how. What's wrong with my trabs, eh?

JONJO. Nothing.

CAIN. But you don't want to copy me, I see. After all I've done for you.

JONJO (*to* RIYAD). S-sorry.

RIYAD. It's cool, fam. I can't even understand what he's saying, to be honest.

CAIN. I want a Coke. Anyone want anything? I've got loads of cartons and that?

RIYAD. Nah, I'm good, man.

CAIN. I'll get you yer favourite. To celebrate.

RIYAD. How you know what my favourite is?

CAIN. I don't but imagine I give yer back a bottle of, like...
Fanta and you were like this *is* my favourite, how sick would
that be? Like, fucking... (*Tries to touch* RIYAD*'s head.*)
ESPN.

> CAIN *gets up and exits unceremoniously. Door reopens
> almost immediately.*

Oh yeah, sound. If I don't come back cus it all gets approved
and all that tell her I said see yer later and... cheers.

See yer later, you fucking whoppers!

RIYAD. Yeah, safe, blud. Go fuck yourself.

> CAIN *exits.*

JONJO. Will they really let him go?

RIYAD. Yeah. People transfer all the time, innit. Move up,
moved out.

JONJO. Right.

RIYAD. Now you won't have to put up with him taking the piss
out of man all the time.

JONJO. At least he talked to me.

RIYAD. He'll be back.

JONJO. I thought you said he was g-g-g...

> RIYAD *waits patiently.*

Getting out?

RIYAD. Yeah, he probably will.

I don't mean come back to this place. But somewhere else
like it, innit. Maybe in a year or two years or whatever.

JONJO. But you said he sh-should try it? You gave him the
letter... back.

RIYAD. Yeah, and he should. He's gonna spend nuff time
behind bars he should take a chance whenever he gets it.

Look… I ain't trying to be a dickhead, yeah? I'm just saying he's textbook, innit? Imagine him in a job interview?

He'll have called the geezer a cunt within two minutes of sitting down.

Bruv… he's alright. Don't say nothing but he's cool with me, I'll back him, yeah, and I'm glad he gets to spend some time with his kid. But bredders like that, it's like they're programmed, when it gets hard, they get shook and come back to what they know, innit.

JONJO. Right.

RIYAD. This is what he knows.

JONJO. Yeah.

RIYAD. Always the way, blud. Trust.

I gotta go link Jake for a minute. Something I need to talk to him about. You all good, yeah?

Yo. You should come play footie with us on a Tuesday. There's just like nine of us right now cus Leon got bumped up so we got a space, innit. Think about it, yeah?

JONJO. D-did you pass your test?

RIYAD. Dunno. Get the results soon. They got to send it to some external… whatnot. I don't even wanna think about it, yano? I done it. Did all the questions and that. I need a seven or something to apply to the college. We'll see, innit.

JONJO. Did you tell your… mum?

RIYAD. Yeah, she was gassed. Proper proud of me, she said. Can't wait for me to come home.

JONJO. That's good. Well done.

RIYAD *puts a hand on* JONJO*'s shoulder.*

RIYAD. I'll see you, innit. Wagwan next week? Grace is gonna have to run through that nappy shit again, still.

Nice kicks, bruv.

RIYAD *exits.*

SEVEN

GRACE, *patient and watchful, waits in the room.*

After a minute, she begins to clear away the things she has laid out for the class.

JONJO *enters.*

JONJO. M-Miss. Sorry I'm late.

GRACE. That's okay. I was beginning to think no one was going to come.

But you're here.

JONJO *nods.*

I was thinking of maybe cancelling it altogether. But then, I thought actually it's probably better that we just… being as we've got a bit of ground to make up.

So, I'll just…

GRACE *begins unpacking the things again.*

Your due date must be coming up soon?

JONJO. My what?

GRACE. Due date? Jess must be nearly full-term now?

JONJO. I dunno, miss.

GRACE. If my maths is correct. Which it often isn't, of course.

JONJO. **,**

GRACE. I couldn't wait to get it over with by that time. I was so uncomfortable. And huge. God. I didn't think it was possible to *balloon* that size. Didn't help that Alex was a summer baby and that year was about the hottest I can remember. Sitting in a car and looking at the dashboard and it was something like thirty-five degrees. Nine months pregnant. I do not recommend it.

He sat very low. And went over by four days.

Did Mr Bradley bring you down?

JONJO. He's waiting outside.

GRACE. Is there anything you wanted to run over… go over again? We could have a bit of a recap session. Anything you're not quite sure about?

JONJO. I dunno, miss.

GRACE. Okay.

JONJO. They won't tell me. Is why I don't know about Jess. Not cus I don't care.

GRACE. Of course.

JONJO. They won't approve her number. So I can't ring her.

GRACE. No.

Well, her parents are probably just a bit worried about her but she'll be able to make her own mind up soon and then maybe… you never know.

JONJO. Yeah.

GRACE. She'll be okay. Try not to worry too much.

JONJO. Can't… help it.

GRACE. No, I know. You're doing everything you can, here.

There was something I wanted to ask you, actually.

JONJO. Right.

GRACE. We might have a new person coming in. Potentially. How would you feel about that?

JONJO. Doing… this?

GRACE. Yeah. He's got an eighteen-month-old girl. He's new here. He was at Cookham Wood before and they didn't have anything like this there and he asked what was involved. His name's Lewis. Have you met him yet?

JONJO. Came in the other week?

GRACE. Yes.

JONJO. With…

GRACE. With Ibrahim. Yes. But they're not friends. He didn't have anything to do with what happened. Obviously. We wouldn't even... but I wanted to sort of, put it to the group first... sort of, gauge a response maybe?

He wouldn't start until next week. Or the week after that, even.

Look, why don't we just do some... something to sort of get our brains going? I mean, we are here. Aren't we? So, we could start with... an exercise –

JONJO. Have you seen him, miss?

GRACE. Seen him?

JONJO. He's not in his room.

GRACE. Oh, of course. No. I haven't.

JONJO. No.

GRACE. I think he's... I think they've moved him for now.

JONJO. M-Moved where?

GRACE. I don't know.

JONJO. What's going to happ–

GRACE. Why don't we just get started?

JONJO. Is he alright?

GRACE. I don't know. I mean, yes. He's fine. He's just... he's in a lot of trouble.

JONJO. They started it. They wanted him to get in trouble. They wanted him to do it.

GRACE. Quite possibly. I don't know the details. Are you okay?

JONJO. I'm... fine.

GRACE. If you need to speak to someone? I can get Jake? Or...

JONJO. He won't tell me anything.

GRACE. No, Jonjo. I meant do you want to talk to Jake about you.

JONJO. I… don't need to.

GRACE. Okay.

JONJO. I need to know what happened to –

GRACE. And I've said I don't know. Jonjo, please. Let's just focus on what we've come to do today and –

JONJO. You *know* he wouldn't. You know he wouldn't have done that –

GRACE. I don't. Actually. I don't know that. I'd like to think so but I don't know that for sure.

It's very serious, what happened. You understand that, don't you?

JONJO. Yes, miss.

GRACE. I'm sorry. I can see it's upset you. I understand why it's upset you. But I shouldn't be talking about it. There are other people dealing with it and we just have to get on, okay?

JONJO. Yes, miss.

GRACE. Okay. Good.

A pause. GRACE, *a little wary.*

Holds out a bag for JONJO.

Can you lay this stuff out for me?

JONJO *takes it.*

Thank you.

JONJO. How many kids you got, miss?

GRACE. Just Alex.

JONJO. Just… Alex.

GRACE. Yeah.

JONJO. Thought you would have had loads.

GRACE. Nope. Just the one. Just Alex.

JONJO. Is he good?

GRACE. Good?

JONJO. Well-behaved.

GRACE. Oh, you know. So-so.

JONJO. So-so?

GRACE. Sometimes. He can be. Very thoughtful. And sweet. And sometimes he makes me want to tear my hair out. But on the whole, he's pretty good, yeah.

JONJO. Not like us.

GRACE. I don't know about that. I think you're pretty good.

CAIN *enters*.

CAIN. Not *very* good though, eh?

GRACE. Cain?

CAIN. We're not very good. No.

GRACE. I didn't have you down for today, Cain.

CAIN. Would you say that? About us?

GRACE. I'm not sure I'd say it about me.

CAIN. Yeah? Done some bad shit, have yer? Smoked a few ciggies when you should have been in school, yeah?

GRACE. Something like that.

CAIN. Am *I* pretty good?

GRACE. Yes, I think so.

CAIN. Is Riyad?

GRACE. ,

CAIN. I was in the paper right, when I was twelve years old. Picture of me. Headline fucking goes… 'Local boy terrorises estate'. Two months later, I got put in here for the first time for mugging some bird of her handbag. Is that good?

GRACE. You were twelve.

CAIN. That make it alright then, does it?

GRACE. Well, I mean, no, but…

CAIN. That what you were doing when you were twelve?

GRACE. No.

CAIN. Robbing people. Hurting 'em.

GRACE. No.

CAIN. You ever smashed the fuck out of someone, eh?

GRACE. No.

CAIN. I mean really fucking bashed 'em up? Stamped on their head, like?

GRACE. No, Cain.

CAIN. Never had to, no?

GRACE. I don't think this is helping, Cain.

CAIN. Oh, is it not? Fucking news to me, that.

GRACE. I've told Jonjo we can't talk about what happened with –

CAIN. What was he supposed to do? Tell me. Let them batter him? Fucking stab him, eh?

GRACE. I don't know.

CAIN. You dunno?

JONJO. They started it.

CAIN. Who cares who fucking started it? It don't matter. He smashed him up. That's all they're gonna see. That's all they're gonna write on the report.

JONJO. We c-could tell them –

CAIN. *W-we c-could tell* 'em. Don't be fucking stupid. Tell 'em what? You think they're gonna listen to you and me?

JONJO *recoils*.

GRACE. Cain, if you're going to stay then we need to continue with the session and I'd like you to just take a brea–

CAIN. Fuck your session!

GRACE. Cain, I'm going to give you a final warning. Unless you take a seat –

CAIN. Even if they didn't start it then, they would've. Sometime. Akeem's been waiting for another one of his boys to get in here, waiting for that Ibby kid, so he had no fucking choice, did he? Either Riyad gets them or they get Riyad. Simple. And he fucking got 'em first. Fair play to the lad.

GRACE. He nearly killed that boy, Cain.

CAIN. No offence, like, but what the fuck do you know about it? About any of this stuff in here? Filling our heads with this fucking… shite. It's alright for you, like. Yeah. Go home to yer nice kid and yer nice house or whatever but what the fuck's he – (*Re:* JONJO.) got? Or any of these lads in here? Like, what the fuck was Riyad gonna do if he went to that college? Do you know what he did to get in here? Do yer?

GRACE. Yes.

CAIN. And you thought he was gonna go and be fucking teacher's pet in that poncey college, yeah? You're more stupid than I am.

JONJO. Don't…

CAIN. He passed them exams. Did yer know that? Got a fucking seven. And for what? What difference has it made? What was the fucking point in doing all that when shit like this just keeps happening. Again and again. Always the fucking same.

JONJO *can't take much more*.

GRACE (*to* JONJO). Jonjo? Do you want me to get Mr Bradley?

CAIN. Telling us we can go off and change our lives and be different but it's just fucking words, isn't it?

GRACE. He could still go. To college. Even if it is later than we thought.

CAIN. You don't understand! You're not listening, are yer? It's – (*Pointing at his head.*) up here that's the fucking problem. It's too late. It's all already fucking happened. And *you* can't change it. You fucking listening?

GRACE. Okay, Cain. Yes.

CAIN. You can't. It always ends up the same.

> And if he fucked it up what chance have I got, eh? I can't do
> them numbers he can do, I can't even fucking read! What the
> fuck do I do out there? If he can't do it, I ain't got no fucking
> chance. I ain't go no chance.

CAIN *runs out of steam.*

GRACE *lets the tension diffuse.*

> Fuck, I could murder a ciggy.

JONJO *gets up, goes over to him and offers him a lollipop.*

Sound.

CAIN *unwraps it. Sucks it.*

> I hate cherry.

JONJO. What's gonna happen?

CAIN. Bang him up for a couple more years. Put him on basic.
No more times tables. No more kid classes.

JONJO (*to* GRACE). He can come back, can't he?

GRACE. It's not up to me.

CAIN. I just came down to say see yer later and that, really.
Surprised Bradley let me, like, but I think Jake had a word
with him so I could. He's alright, like.

JONJO. So, you are going?

CAIN. Riyad was always going on about it, weren't he, and it's
all booked in now so they'd be proper mardy with me if
I didn't go now.

> Sorry about the... you know. Just fucking boring in here.
> I never meant nothing by it.

JONJO. I could write to you.

CAIN. Alright, Meg Ryan, calm down. Don't be gay about it.
What we gonna be? Fucking penpals? Anyway, let's be
honest I couldn't fucking read it, cus I'm a spaz.

JONJO. But you've got dyslexia?

CAIN. Yeah. That's what I said, didn't I?

Just remember to give Ry or one of the new lads a slap every once in a while, so they don't get ideas –

GRACE. Cain...

CAIN. I'm giving advice!

Hope your mum comes, mate.

They look for a second like they might hug.

They don't.

GRACE. They'll be wondering where you've got to.

CAIN. Yeah, right.

Listen, if you see Riyad, like, tell him... tell him I said sound, right? I wouldn't be doing this if he hadn't banged on about it and everything so if you could just let him know, like, that I...

GRACE. I'll tell him.

CAIN. Nice one. See yer, Grace.

CAIN *exits.*

(*Off.*) Zahid, yer nonce. Took you twelve weeks to make that? What the fuck even is it?

GRACE. Alright?

JONJO. Ye-Yes.

GRACE. At least he's not going to run out of energy, anyway. I think his son will probably struggle to keep up with him.

JONJO. Yeah.

Can I have a h-hug, miss?

GRACE. No.

JONJO. ,

GRACE. I'm not allowed. You know that.

JONJO. Right, miss.

GRACE. Jake's in his office if you'd wanted to talk to someone about –

JONJO. No. That's okay.

Can we do ch-changing again? I've sort of...

GRACE. Yeah, of course. Look, I've got to go and talk to Jake. Just a quick word. So, why don't you set up for me and then when I come back we get started, okay?

JONJO. Okay.

GRACE. You know where everything is, don't you?

JONJO. Yeah.

GRACE. Okay. I'll just be a sec.

GRACE *exits.*

JONJO *takes out a baby doll. Some nappies.*

Picks up the baby doll. Cradles it.

The End.

A Nick Hern Book

Shook first published in Great Britain as a paperback original in 2019 by Nick Hern Books Limited, The Glasshouse, 49a Goldhawk Road, London W12 8QP, in association with Papatango Theatre Company

Front cover: photograph of Jake Morton Miles by Michael Wharley; image design by Rebecca Pitt

Designed and typeset by Nick Hern Books, London
Printed in the UK by Mimeo Ltd, Huntingdon, Cambridgeshire PE29 6XX

A CIP catalogue record for this book is available from the British Library

ISBN 978 1 84842 894 2

www.nickhernbooks.co.uk

 facebook.com/nickhernbooks

 twitter.com/nickhernbooks